101
3-4 STUNTS

LEO HAND

ISBN: 1-58518-700-3
Library of Congress Control Number: 2002108118
Cover design: Jennifer Bokelmann
Diagrams and Layout: Deborah Oldenburg
Front cover photo: Matthew Stockman/Allsport

Coaches Choice
PO Box 1828
Monterey, CA 93942
www.coacheschoice.com

DEDICATION

FOR MARY

AND OUR SEVEN GRANDCHILDREN:
FAITH, MIKAYLA, ADAM, ERIC,
ETHAN, OWEN, and TRAVIS.

ACKNOWLEDGMENTS

Thanks to Tony Shaw for giving me the opportunity to coach in Texas.

Thanks to Jim Murphy, Don Kloppenberg, and Will Shaw for all they taught me about defense at Long Beach City College.

Thanks to the wonderful people of the Zuni and Navajo Nations who taught me much more than I taught them during the seven years I lived with them.

Thanks to Joe Griffin for giving me one of the best coaching jobs in California.

Thanks to all of the splendid young men whom I have been privileged to coach.

Thanks to all of the great coaches whom I have been fortunate to have worked with and coached against.

Thanks to Phil Johnson for all of his help and kind words.

Thanks to Conrado Ronquillo, Joe Barba, and the maintenance crew at Irvin High School for all of their patience, kindness and help during this project.

Thanks to Sam Snoddy for his assistance during this project

Thanks to the offspring whose ancestors endured the *Middle Chamber* and the *Long Walk* for all of the contributions that they have made to the greatest game of all.

Thanks to Howard Wells for giving me the chance to coach at El Paso High School.

Thanks to Herman Masin, editor of Scholastic Coach, for all of his help and suggestions during the past 30 years.

Thanks to Dr. James A. Peterson for all of his help and encouragement.

CONTENTS

INTRODUCTION

BEFORE WE BEGIN

There are a few terms that will constantly be referred to throughout the text. Because different phrases and words can sometimes mean different things to different people, the following terms are defined and clarified as they are used in this book:

- **Strongside/weakside:** The strongside is toward the tight end, and the weakside is toward the split end. Strong defenders (example: strong tackle) are aligned on the tight-end side, and weak defenders are aligned on the split-end side.
- **Player position names** are as illustrated in Figure Intro-1:

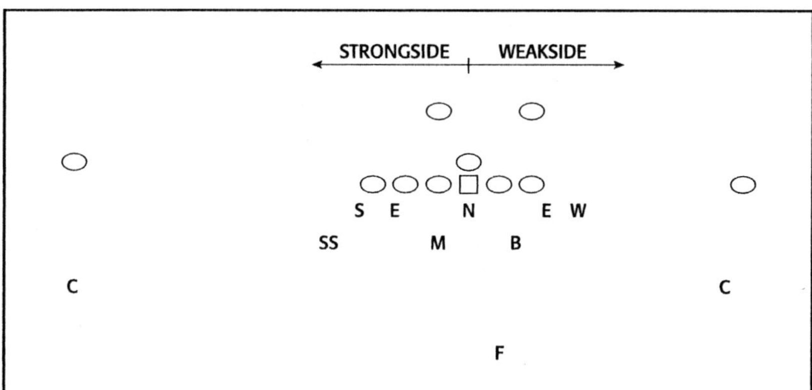

Figure Intro-1

Strong cornerback–the cornerback who lines up opposite the flanker.

Weak cornerback–the cornerback who lines up opposite the split end.

Strong safety–the safety who lines up on the strongside.

Weak safety–the safety who lines up on the weakside.

Stud–the outside linebacker who lines up toward the strongside.

Strong end–the defensive end who lines up on the strongside.

Mike–the inside linebacker aligned on the strongside.

Nose–the defensive lineman who lines up opposite the center.

Buck–the inside linebacker aligned on the weakside.

Weak end–the defensive end who lines up on the weakside.

Whip–the outside linebacker who lines up on the weakside.

- **Gap responsibilities** are lettered as illustrated in Figure Intro-2:

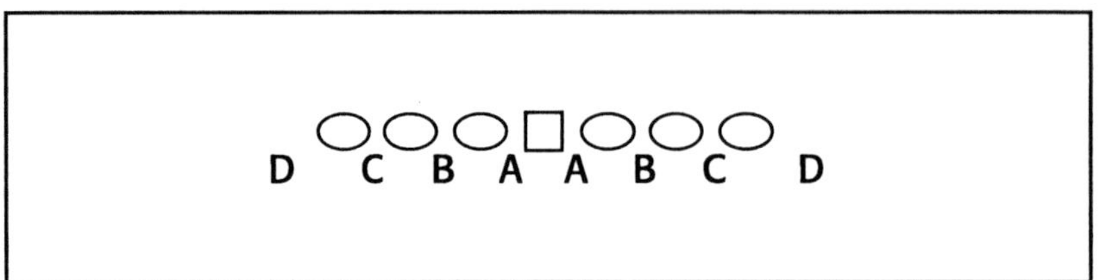

Figure Intro-2

- **Alignments** are numbered as illustrated in Figure Intro-3:

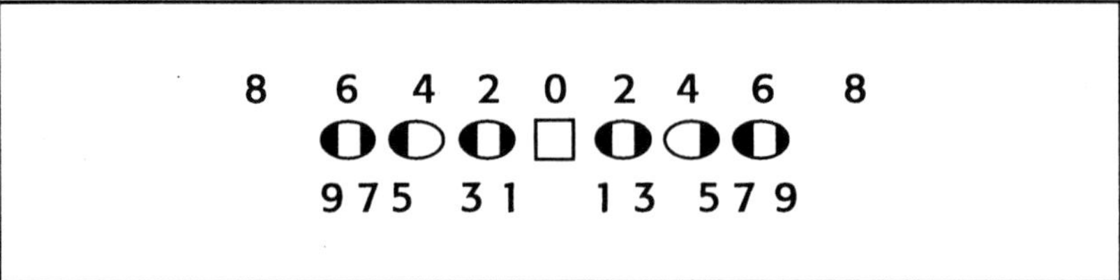

Figure Intro-3

- **Receivers** are numbered as illustrated in Figure Intro-4:

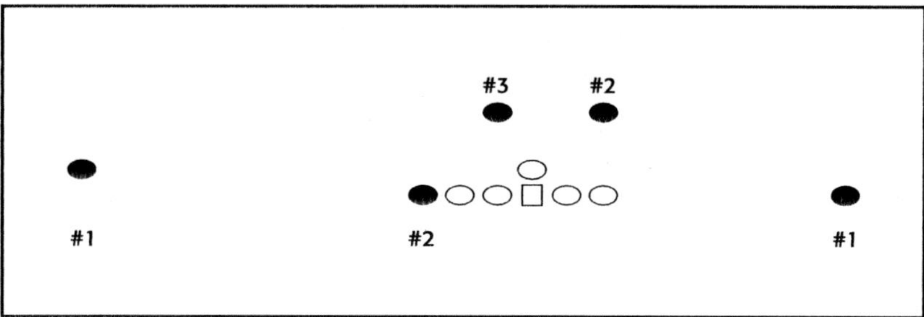

Figure Intro-4

BASE TECHNIQUES

To avoid needlessly repeating the player assignments when explaining stunts, the base assignments and techniques for each defender aligned in the box are reviewed in this section.

- **0 Technique (Nose)**

  This player lines up opposite the center. He is responsible for both A gaps. First, he keys the center and then both guards. He controls the center's block and protects the flow-side A gap. If the guards and center scoop block, he attacks the center and prevents him from blocking a linebacker. If the guard double-teams him, he must not get driven back. Pulling guards usually indicate a play's direction. He should pursue through the A gap.

- **Deep 3 Technique (Mike and Buck)**

  This player lines up outside shade on the guard. He controls the B gap. First, he keys the guard and then the tackle. If the guard tries to block him, he quickly approaches the line and attacks the guard as close to the line as possible. If the guard blocks the 0 technique, and the tackle blocks the 5 technique, the play is an iso. The 3-technique player plugs the hole quickly and takes on the lead back with an inside forearm rip. He keeps his outside arm and leg free and maintains outside leverage. If the guard blocks the 0 technique, and the tackle blocks the 3-technique player, the play is a trap. The defender should fill off the tail of the defensive end, who should be closing inside. If the guard pulls outside, and the tackle cracks down on the 3-technique player, he fights the pressure, and pursues the ball from an inside-out position. If the guard pulls inside, the defender pursues from an inside-out position and watches for counter and cutback.

- **5 Technique (Defensive Ends)**

  This player lines up outside shade on the tackle. He steps with his inside foot and controls the C gap. First, he keys the tackle and then the tight end. He fights the pressure of the tackle's block. If the tackle blocks inside, but the 5-technique player feels no pressure from the tight end, the play is a trap—"trap the trapper." If the tackle blocks inside, and the tight end cracks down on the player, he fights outside pressure and controls the C gap. If he's double-teamed, he attacks the tight end and makes sure he's not driven back.

- **9 Technique (Stud and Whip)**

  This player plays outside shade on the tight end. If there isn't a tight end, he lines up three to five feet outside of the offensive tackle and three yards deep.. First he keys the tight end, then the near back, and then a pulling lineman. He steps with his inside foot, and doesn't let the tight end hook him. Versus sweep, he controls the tight end's block, maintains outside leverage, and tries to get upfield and force the ball inside or wide and deep. If the tight end blocks inside, he squeezes the C gap and looks for the near back to kick him out. If this doesn't happen, he looks for an offensive lineman to trap him. He attacks the blocker and dumps the play inside. The 9-technique player should keep his outside leg free, and be prepared for the back to break the play outside. If the tight end releases outside, he first looks to the near back and then to a pulling lineman. He should be prepared to be kicked out, hooked, or logged.

CHAPTER 1

NEW DEFENSIVE STRATEGIES

In recent years, defensive coaches have developed a number innovative strategies that have made pass blocking a chaotic guessing game, destroyed the reliability of hot reads, and limited the number of pass receivers an offense can put into a pattern and still safely protect the quarterback. Most of these new strategies involve the tactic of illusion. When employing an *illusion* scheme, seven or eight defenders will attack the line of scrimmage at the snap and give the offense the *illusion* of a total blitz. Once the defense reads pass, however, only a pre-determined number of defenders will continue to rush the quarterback. The remaining *fake blitzers* will either *spy* the running backs or drop off into coverage. To compound the offensive problem even further, the *fake blitzers* may be defensive linemen. Therefore, the offense never knows (until it is too late) how many or which defenders will rush the quarterback. Every defender aligned in the box is now both a potential pass rusher or a coverage player. Modern offenses must account for each and every player in the box. *Illusion* gives the defense a tremendous advantage over the offense and is not only an effective passing game deterrent, but it's also proven to be deadly versus the run. If, in future years, offensive teams try to counter *illusion* tactics by employing formations that feature no running backs, they will become one dimensional, and whenever an offense becomes one dimensional, it becomes easier to defend.

ELEVEN INNOVATIVE STUNT TACTICS

- **Illusion Stunts**

  Illusion stunts are the grandparents of the entire defensive revolution. Figure 1-1 shows eight defenders attacking the line at the snap. The offense's dilemma is trying to figure out which defenders are *spying* the two running backs—the outside linebackers, or the ends. If the offense tries to release the tight end and one or two running backs, it must attempt to block the *illusion* of an 8-on-6 or 8-on-5 mismatch, which could result in one, two, or three unblocked defenders chasing the quarterback. In this situation, the quarterback may be able to beat the sack, but he'll often end up throwing off balance, making a bad decision, and/or getting picked.

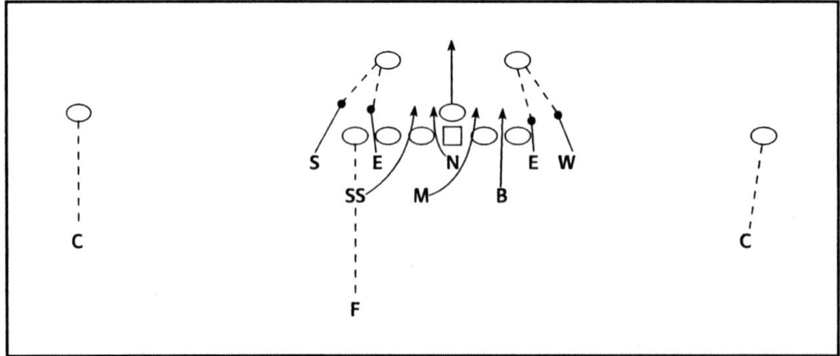

Figure 1-1

- **Banjo Blitzes**

  Most coaches refer to this tactic as a *zone blitz* or *fire zone blitz*. I call it *banjo* for several reasons. One reason is because when I first saw the tactic, it reminded me of the old inside-out-combo coverage, traditionally called banjo, that has been around for years. Another reason is because the cornerbacks are playing man, not zone. Back when Tom Bass was coaching in the NFL, he was blitzing linebackers and dropping linemen into pass coverage. Because every defender dropping into coverage was employing zone techniques, Tom called the tactic *zone blitz*. Because I learned both the tactic and its name from Tom, I had to give the "new zone blitz" another name—*banjo*. Two innovations have been added to the old *banjo* concept to create the new scheme. First, a third defender has been added to the *banjo* scheme, and secondly, defensive linemen are now dropping off into *banjo* coverage. In Figure 1-2, all of the linebackers are blitzing. The strong safety, the nose, and the weak end are employing base reads versus run and then dropping into a specific area when they read pass. The defenders dropping into an area are jointly responsible for covering the tight end and two running backs. Each defender is therefore responsible for covering any of these three receivers if they enter his area. I will refer to the three *banjo* areas into which the defenders drop as: Abel, Baker, and Charlie.

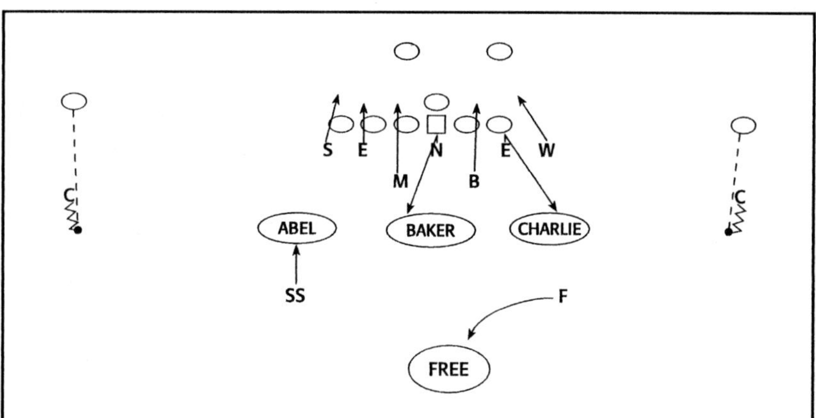

Figure 1-2

- **Gumbo Blitzes**

  This tactic is very similar to the old banjo concept in which two strongside defenders combo-covered the tight end and the strongside halfback by themselves. What's new about gumbo is that a weakside *illusion* is being employed and one defender is *spying* the weakside halfback instead of being assigned straight man coverage. Like *banjo*, *gumbo* holds the offense accountable for blocking all of the potential pass rushers in the box. It also causes offensive linemen to frequently end up blocking "air," and eliminates double-read pass-blocking schemes.

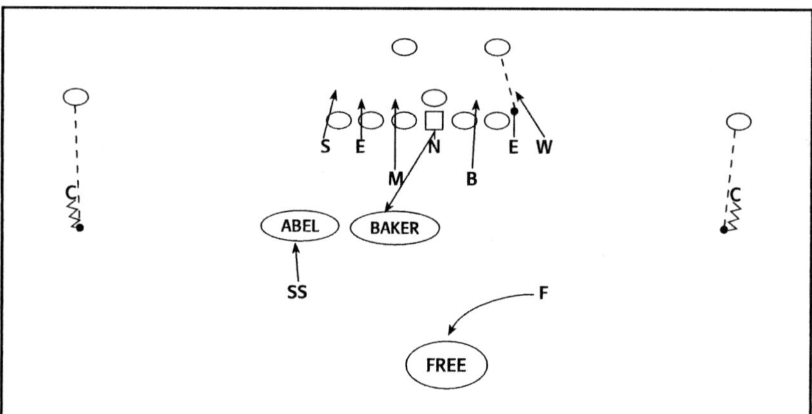

Figure 1-3

- **Zone Blitzes**

  This tactic closely resembles the zone blitz of Tom Bass. Figure 1-4 shows the nose, normally a rusher when cover 3 is employed, dropping into coverage. Conversely, the two inside linebackers and Whip, who are normally coverage players, are now blitzing.

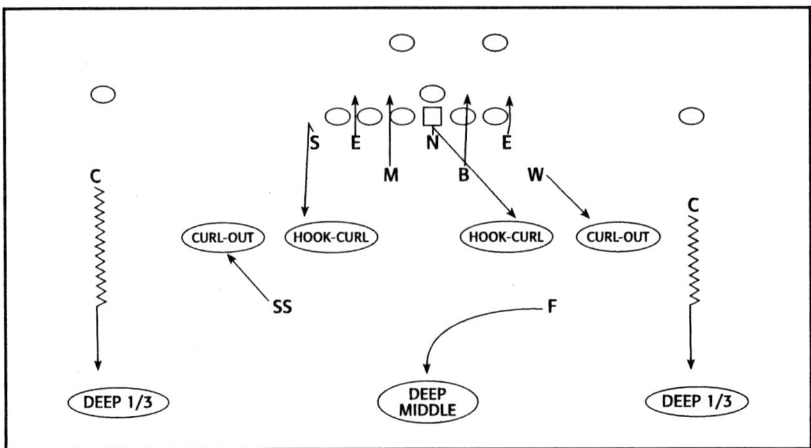

Figure 1-4

- **Delayed Overloads**

  Overload blitzes always have been, and always will be, an extremely effective defensive tactic. Overloads attempt to get more pass rushers on one side of the ball than available offensive pass blockers. Figure 1-5 shows an overload with four strongside pass rushers. The only way that the offense can handle this overload is to use both their tight end and strongside halfback as pass blockers. The stunt begins as a strongside *illusion* with Stud *spying* the halfback. Buck employs a base read technique versus run, but once he reads pass, he delay blitzes through the B gap.

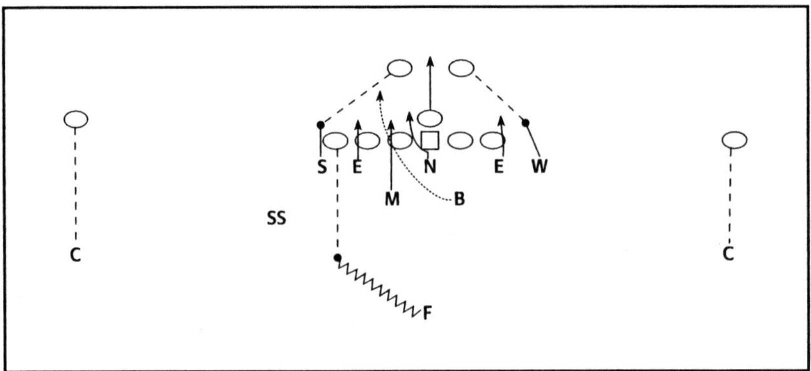

Figure 1-5

- **Line/Linebacker Twists**

  Line/linebacker twists are particularly effective versus man pass-blocking assignments. They also enable six or seven defenders to drop off into coverage. Figure 1-6 shows a double delayed twist that is being employed from a 4-under/2-deep zone. The nose and Whip are employing base techniques versus run, but executing a delayed twist once they read pass. Stud and the strong end are also employing base techniques versus run, and twisting once they read pass. There is, of course, another type of line twist in which the defenders will immediately twist at the snap of the ball. These immediate twists are generally more effective versus the run, while the delayed twists are more effective versus the pass. Line twists are often combined with linebacker blitzes to intensify the pressure of the stunt.

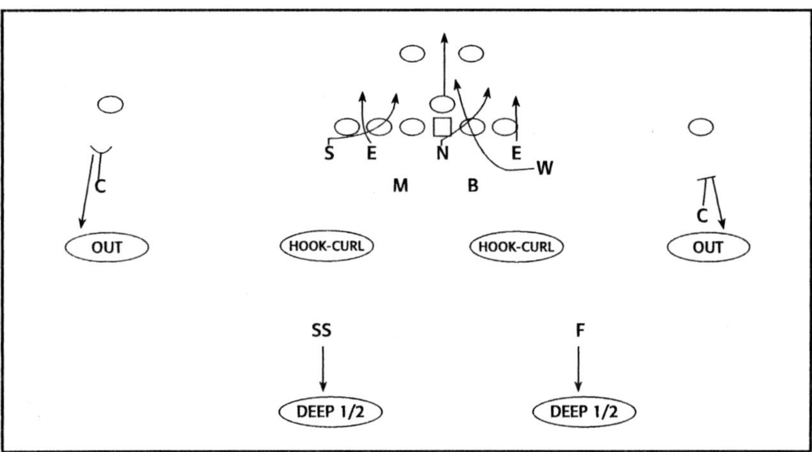

Figure 1-6

- **Dogs**

  Most coaches refer to 5-man rushes as dogs. This is an "old school" tactic that is frequently used with cover 1, because it enables a defense to drop six players. Figure 1-7 shows both outside linebackers blitzing and the two inside backers covering the near backs.

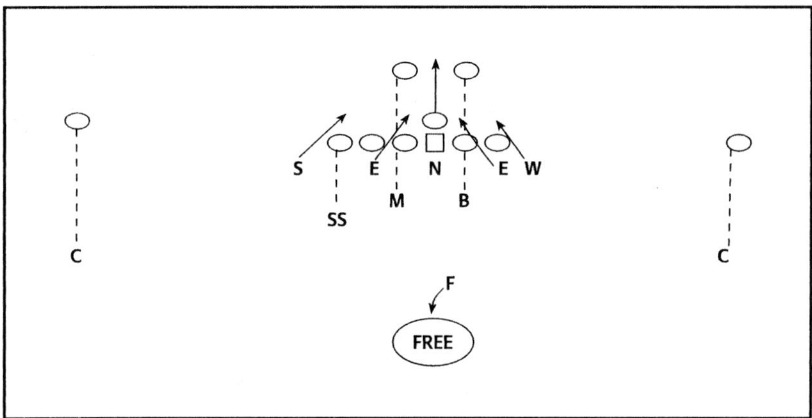

Figure 1-7

- **Blitzes**

  Any 6-man rush is generally referred to as a blitz. These are more risky than dogs, because the defense is not afforded the luxury of a free safety. In Figure 1-8, the free safety and Stud are covering the two running backs, and the strong safety is assigned the tight end.

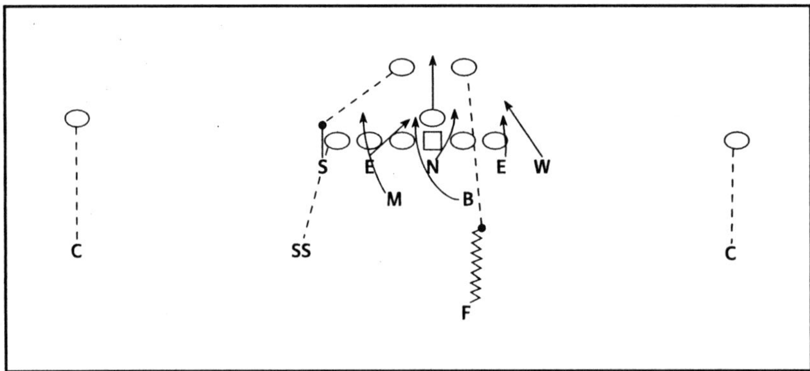

Figure 1-8

- **Flow Dogs**

  A flow dog is another "old school" tactic. In Figures 1-9a through 1-9c, both inside linebackers are assigned to blitz, but where they will blitz is predicated upon the backfield flow.

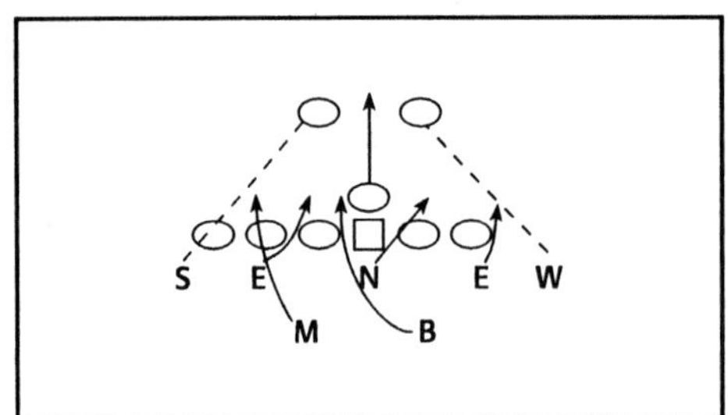

Figure 1-9a

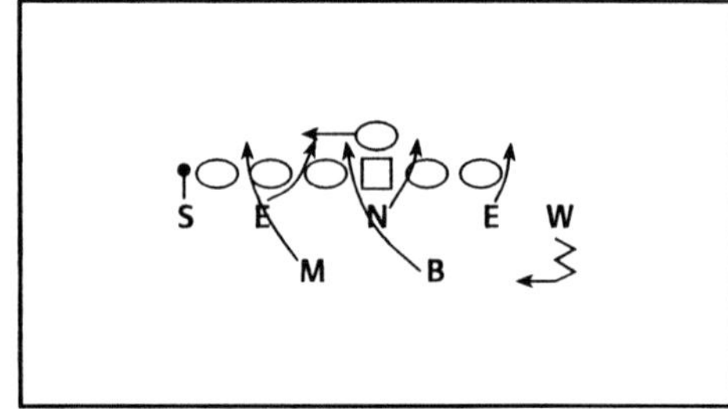

Figure 1-9b

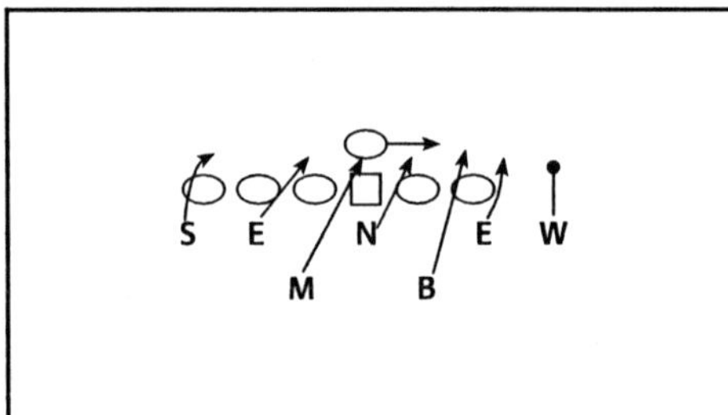

Figure 1-9c

- **Secondary Blitzes**

  Secondary blitzes and fake secondary blitzes are powerful, multifaceted weapons. Figure 1-10 shows a strong cornerback blitz, using a variation of cover 1 banjo.

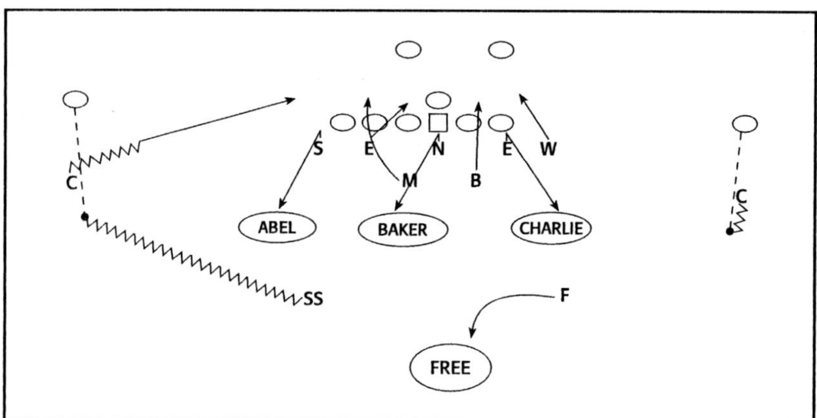

Figure 1-10

- **Twin Stunts**

  Whenever two players are assigned to stunt through the same gap, it is referred to as a *twin stunt*. In Figure 1-11, both Stud and Mike are stunting through the B gap. This is an unusual tactic. Since few offensive teams ever see this type of stunt, it is often very effective. Twin stunts are usually called in passing situations.

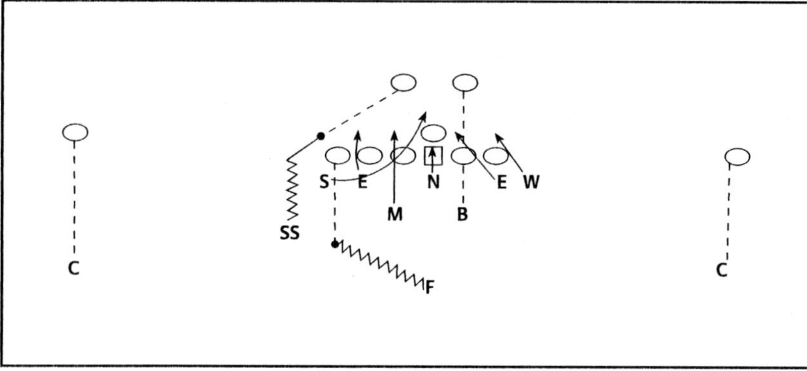

Figure 1-11

CHAPTER 2

BASIC PRINCIPLES OF BLITZING

- If a player blitzes infrequently, using it as an element of surprise, it's important that he disguises his intention.
- If a player frequently blitzes, disguising his intention may not be as important because he may want to occasionally give the offense a false key by *showing blitz* but then *playing straight* at the snap of the ball. Whichever strategy he decides to use, it is important that he does not establish a pattern that can be exploited.
- A player's eyes are one of his most important tools when blitzing. To be an effective blitzer, a player must be able to see (on the run) the keys that will lead him to the ball. Seeing these keys is the first step in being able to read and react to them.
- Unless the blitz is a delayed reaction to a pass, it is critical that the blitzer is moving, attacking, and penetrating the line of scrimmage at the snap of the ball.
- A blitzer must keep his feet moving at all times. This factor is especially important when he becomes engaged with a blocker.
- A blitzing player should use his quickness to avoid blockers.

- If the play is a pass, and the blitzer becomes engaged with a blocker, he should keep his hands inside of the blocker's hands and try to maintain separation from the blocker. He should not look at the passer too soon, or he may lose sight of the blocker. The blitzer must first defeat the blocker before he can sack the quarterback. While a blitzing player should have a predetermined pass rush move in mind, he should be ready to change his move according to the circumstances. A blitzer needs to take what the blocker gives him and make his move at the appropriate time. Remember that if a blitzing player makes his pass rush move too soon, the blocker will have time to recover. On the other hand, if he makes his move too late, he will probably be too close to the blocker, thereby enabling the blocker to get into the blitzer's body and nullify his charge. If possible, the blitzer should try to get the blocker turned one way and then make his move in the opposite direction. The blitzing player should also use his forward momentum to manipulate the blocker's momentum. If the blocker's momentum is back, the blitzer should attack him with a power move and knock him backwards. If his momentum is forward, the player can use a move that puts the blocker forward and destroys his balance. A blitzing player should never leave his feet to bat a ball down. He should get his hands up as the quarterback begins his throwing motion, but continue his charge toward the quarterback. Too often, when a defender jumps up to bat a pass down, the quarterback will duck under, elude the defender, and scramble out of the pocket.
- If the play is a run, a blitzer should react to his keys and the pressure of blocks as he normally would if he were employing a read technique. Since a blitzer has forward momentum to his advantage, he should use his hands rather than his forearm when attacking a blocker. A blitzing player must maintain separation from blockers and not let them get into his legs. If possible, blitzers should try to make the blocker miss.
- When blitzing, a player should keep his body under control at all times, try to maintain a low center of gravity and provide as small a target as possible for the blockers.
- Blitzers need to study their opponents' game films carefully. They should know how their potential blockers react and what techniques they favor. It helps to know the strengths and weaknesses of the opponent.
- A blitzer should also study his opponent's eyes as he's getting set at the line of scrimmage. The blocker's eyes will often tell a blitzer where he's going. Studying the pressure that the blocker puts on his down hand when he gets into his stances will also frequently give a pass/run or directional key. .
- Blitzers who study the scouting report will increase their knowledge of the opponents' formation, down-and-distance, and field-position tendencies. They should use this information to anticipate, but never to guess.

- All players should gang tackle and try to strip the ball out of the ballcarrier's arm. Players should never take for granted that a running back or quarterback has been downed. If they arrive at a pile late, they should be on the alert for a loose ball.
- Players must maintain total intensity from the time the ball is snapped until the whistle is blown.
- Before the snap, a blitzer should anticipate potential blockers and be prepared to react to those blockers as he penetrates the line.
- On plays directed toward a blitzer's side of the field, he should make the tackle. On plays directed away from him, he should take the proper angle of pursuit and be in on the tackle. Players should always pursue relentlessly. Remember that if a player is not within five yards of the ball when the whistle blows he is probably loafing.
- If the backfield action does not indicate flow, a blitzer should protect his gap until he finds the ball. He should never guess.
- If a player is assigned to *spy* (cover a back) when he's blitzing, he should expect that the back will first block and then run a delayed route. Do not allow him to be fooled. Remind him that he must cover the back, no matter what the back does, until the whistle blows.
- The ball is the blitzer's trigger. When the ball is snapped, *he's gone!* He should not listen to an opponent's cadence; they're not talking to him!
- Players should not rely upon the lines that are marked on the field. The ball, not the lines, establishes the line of scrimmage.

CHAPTER 3

ZERO COVERAGE STUNTS

When zero coverage is employed, there will be no free safeties. The three defensive backs will be assigned to guard the tight end and two wide receivers man-to-man. One or two defenders in the box will be assigned to cover the two running backs, and the fourth defensive back will either be sent on a blitz or assigned to cover one of the running backs.

The strength of the zero coverage strategy is that it has eight defenders in the vicinity of the box, attacking gaps and penetrating the line of scrimmage. Its weakness is that all of the secondary defenders are locked on receivers and none are keying the ball; therefore, if a runner breaks the line of scrimmage or a defensive back gets beat deep, there is a good chance that a touchdown will result. Despite this weakness, zero coverage can cause an offense a lot of problems, especially when the defenders in the box have some "quicks," and the defensive backs are skillful man-to-man pass defenders.

SECONDARY MAN-TO-MAN TECHNIQUES FOR ZERO COVERAGE

Stance and Alignment

A defensive secondary player should:

- Align himself with an inside shade on the receiver, approximately seven yards deep.
- Set up with a narrow base, feet inside of his arm-pits, outside foot up (toe-heel relationship).
- Keep his weight on his front foot.
- Keep his knees bent and his hips lowered.
- Slightly round his back with his head and shoulders over his front foot (nose over the toes).
- Allow his arms to hang loose.
- See both the receiver and the quarterback with his peripheral vision.

Backpedal

A defensive secondary player should:

- Maintain inside leverage on the receiver.
- Keep a good forward lean as he backpedals (chin down and nose over the toes).
- Push off with his front foot and take his first step with his back foot. He should not step forward or lift a foot and set it back down in the same place.
- Keep his weight on the balls of his feet.
- Reach back with each step and pull his weight over his feet.
- Keep his feet close to the ground during the backpedal.
- Not over stride; take small-to-medium steps.
- Keep his arms bent at a 90-degree angle - relaxed, but pumping vigorously.
- Maintain a proper cushion. When the receiver gets 10 yards downfield, the defender should be 15 yards deep. When the receiver is 15 yards downfield, the defender should be 18 yards deep.
- Remember and anticipate that 3-step routes are usually thrown five to seven yards downfield (the exception being the fade); 5-step patterns are thrown 12 to 15 yards downfield; and 7-step routes are usually thrown 18+ yards downfield.
- Be aware of a receiver's split. Wide splits often indicate inside routes; tight splits often indicate outside routes.

- Keep his shoulders parallel to the line and not let the receiver turn him.
- Mirror the receiver's movements while keeping his own outside shoulder on the receiver's inside shoulder. He must not let the receiver get head up with him.
- Control the speed of his backpedal. When the receiver makes his break, the defender must be under control and able to gather and break quickly in the direction of the break.
- Concentrate on the base of the receiver's numbers until he makes his final break.
- Anticipate a break when the receiver changes his forward lean, begins to chop his feet, or begins to widen his base.
- Honor all inside fakes.
- Not backpedal at the snap if aligned on a tight end. Be ready to jump a flat or crossing route. If the tight end goes vertical, the defender must work to an inside-leverage position.
- Remember that "if the receiver gets even (with the defender), he's leavin'." Whenever a receiver gets too close, the defender must turn and run with him, keeping his body between the receiver and the ball. He must not allow separation to occur. As he's running with the receiver, he can try to disrupt the receiver's strides by slapping at his near hand and wrist.

Plant and Drive

- When the receiver makes his final break, the defensive back should drop his shoulder in the direction of the receiver's break and explode in that direction. He must make his break parallel to the receiver's break and quickly close the cushion.
- The defender must not lose concentration on the receiver. He should not look for the ball until he's closed his cushion, and he sees the receiver look for the ball.
- If the receiver tries to change direction after the defender has begun his drive, the defensive player should be in a position so that the receiver will have to make contact with him in order to change directions.

Playing the Ball

A defensive secondary player should:

- Attack the ball at its highest point.
- Play the ball, not the receiver, when the ball is to his inside and the receiver is outside of him.
- Play the ball through the receiver's upfield shoulder when the receiver is between him and the ball. He should never cut in front of the receiver to make an

interception unless he is absolutely sure that he can get two hands on the ball.

- Try to catch the ball or break up a pass with two hands, not one.
- Always knock the ball toward the ground, never up in the air.
- Try to strip the ball if the receiver catches the pass.
- Head to the nearest sideline when he intercepts a pass.
- Always look the ball into his hands and protect it after he catches it.

STUNT #1

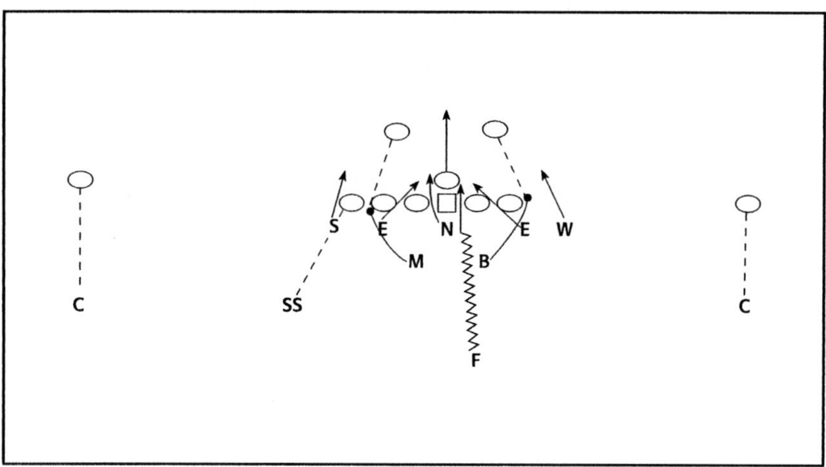

STUNT DESCRIPTION: This free safety blitz is an **illusion** stunt that gives the offense the illusion of an eight-man pass rush.

SECONDARY COVERAGE: Zero coverage. Mike and Buck spy the near backs, and the strong safety covers the tight end. Possible variation: Stud and Whip spy the near backs.

STRONG SAFETY: Covers the tight end.

STUD: Rushes from the outside. Contains strongside run and pass. Chases weakside run.

STRONG END: Slants into and controls the B gap.

MIKE: Stunts to the C gap. Spies the near back.

NOSE: Slants to and controls the strongside A gap.

BUCK: Stunts to the C gap. Spies the near back.

WEAK END: Slants into and controls the B gap.

WHIP: Rushes from the outside. Contains strongside run and pass. Chases weakside run.

FREE SAFETY: Blitzes through the weakside A gap.

STRONG CORNER: Covers receiver #1 (inside technique).

WEAK CORNER: Covers receiver #1 (inside technique).

STUNT #2

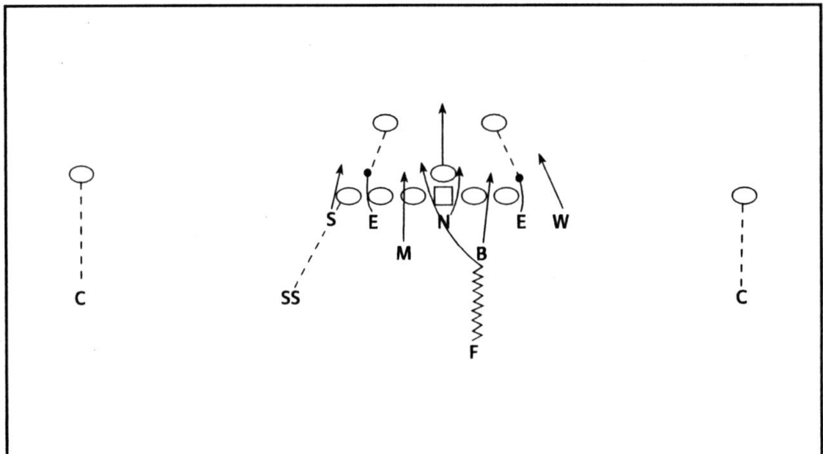

STUNT DESCRIPTION: This free safety blitz is an **illusion** stunt that gives the offense the illusion of an eight-man pass rush.

SECONDARY COVERAGE: Zero coverage. The two ends spy the near backs, and the strong safety covers the tight end. Possible variation: Stud and Whip spy the near backs.

STRONG SAFETY: Covers the tight end.

STUD: Rushes from the outside. Contains strongside run and pass. Chases weakside run.

STRONG END: Plays 5 technique versus run. Spies the near back versus pass.

MIKE: Blitzes through the outside shoulder of the offensive guard. Controls the B gap.

NOSE: Slants to and controls the weakside A gap.

BUCK: Blitzes through the outside shoulder of the offensive guard. Controls the B gap.

WEAK END: Plays 5 technique versus run. Spies the near back versus pass.

WHIP: Rushes from the outside. Contains strongside run and pass. Chases weakside run.

FREE SAFETY: Approaches the line during cadence to make it look as though a weakside blitz is in progress. As the ball is snapped, he blitzes through the strongside A gap.

STRONG CORNER: Covers receiver #1 (inside technique).

WEAK CORNER: Covers receiver #1 (inside technique).

STUNT #3

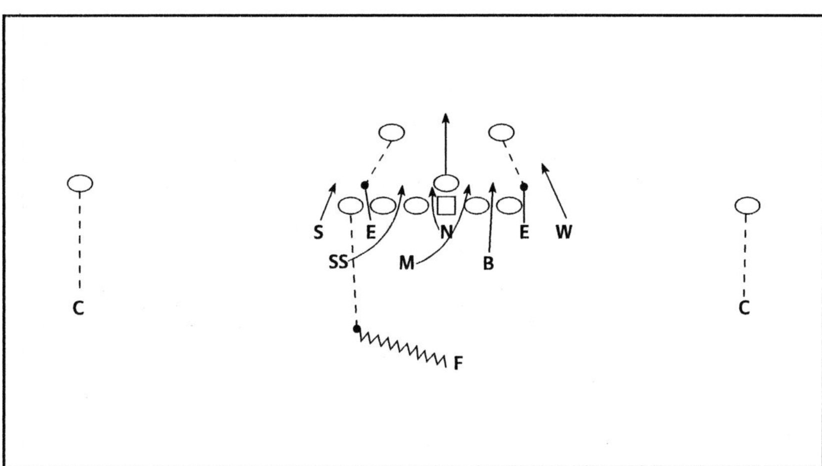

STUNT DESCRIPTION: This strong safety blitz is an **illusion** stunt that gives the offense the illusion of an eight-man pass rush.

SECONDARY COVERAGE: Zero coverage. The two ends spy the near backs, and the free safety covers the tight end. Possible variation: Stud and Whip spy the near backs.

STRONG SAFETY: Lines up inside shade on the tight end, four to five yards deep. Blitzes through the B gap.

STUD: Rushes from the outside. Contains strongside run and pass. Chases weakside run.

STRONG END: Plays 5 technique versus run. Spies the near back versus pass.

MIKE: Blitzes through the weakside A gap.

NOSE: Slants to and controls the strongside A gap.

BUCK: Blitzes through the outside shoulder of the offensive guard and controls the B gap.

WEAK END: Plays 5 technique versus run. Spies the near back versus pass.

WHIP: Rushes from the outside. Contains strongside run and pass. Chases weakside run.

FREE SAFETY: Covers the tight end. Disguises his assignment as though he's playing cover 1 and slowly creeps into position as the quarterback calls cadence.

STRONG CORNER: Covers receiver #1 (inside technique).

WEAK CORNER: Covers receiver #1 (inside technique).

STUNT #4

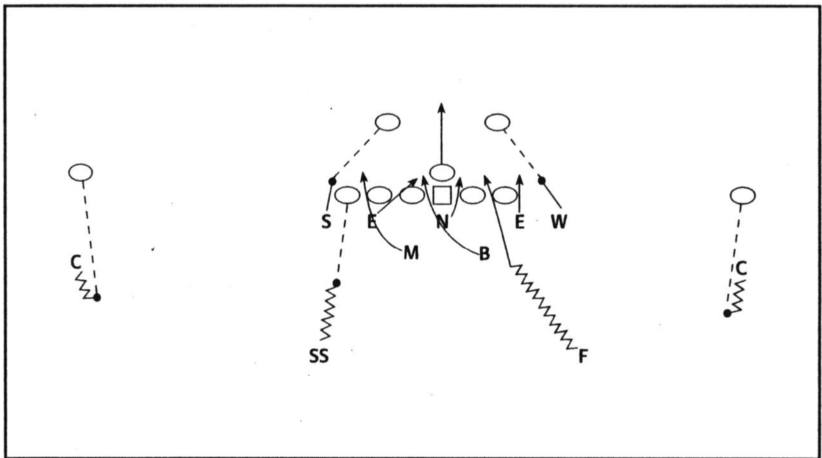

STUNT DESCRIPTION: This free-safety blitz is an **illusion** stunt that gives the offense the illusion of an eight-man pass rush.

SECONDARY COVERAGE: Zero coverage. Stud and Whip spy the near backs, and the strong safety covers the tight end. Possible variation: Mike and the weakside end spy the near backs.

STRONG SAFETY: Covers the tight end. Disguises his assignment as cover 2 and slowly creeps into position as the quarterback calls cadence.

STUD: Rushes from the outside. Contains strongside run and chases weakside run. Spies the near back versus pass.

STRONG END: Slants into and controls the B gap.

MIKE: Blitzes through the C gap. Secures the C gap versus run and contains the quarterback.

NOSE: Slants to the weakside A gap.

BUCK: Blitzes through the strongside A gap.

WEAK END: Plays 5 technique.

WHIP: Rushes from the outside. Contains strongside run and chases weakside run. Spies the near back versus pass.

FREE SAFETY: Disguises his assignment as though he's playing cover 2. As the quarterback calls cadence, free safety creeps toward the line and blitzes through the weakside B gap.

STRONG CORNER: Covers receiver #1 (inside technique disguised as cover 2 man).

WEAK CORNER: Covers receiver #1 (inside technique disguised as cover 2 man).

STUNT #5

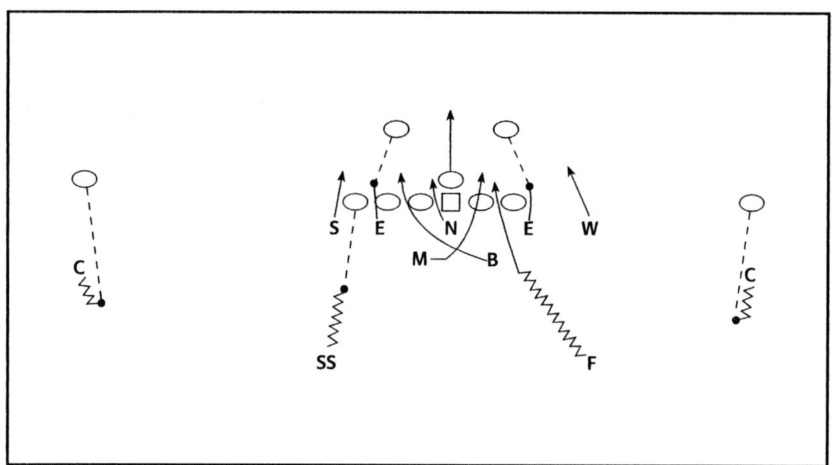

STUNT DESCRIPTION: This free-safety blitz is an **illusion** stunt that gives the offense the illusion of an eight-man pass rush.

SECONDARY COVERAGE: Zero coverage. Both ends spy the near backs, and the strong safety covers the tight end. Possible variation: Stud and Whip spy the near backs.

STRONG SAFETY: Covers the tight end. Disguises his assignment as cover 2 and slowly creeps into position as the quarterback calls cadence.

STUD: Rushes from the outside. Contains strongside run and pass. Chases weakside run.

STRONG END: Plays 5 technique. Spies the near back versus pass.

MIKE: Blitzes through the weakside A gap. Buck goes first. Mike's first step is a short jab step parallel to the line with his right foot.

NOSE: Slants to the strongside A gap.

BUCK: Blitzes through the strongside B gap. Buck goes first. His first step should be directly at his aiming point.

WEAK END: Plays 5 technique. Spies the near back versus pass.

WHIP: Rushes from the outside. Contains strongside run and pass. Chases weakside run.

FREE SAFETY: Disguises his assignment as though he's playing cover 2. As the quarterback calls cadence, the free safety creeps toward the line and blitzes through the weakside B gap.

STRONG CORNER: Covers receiver #1 (inside technique disguised as cover 2 man).

WEAK CORNER: Covers receiver #1 (inside technique disguised as cover 2 man).

STUNT #6

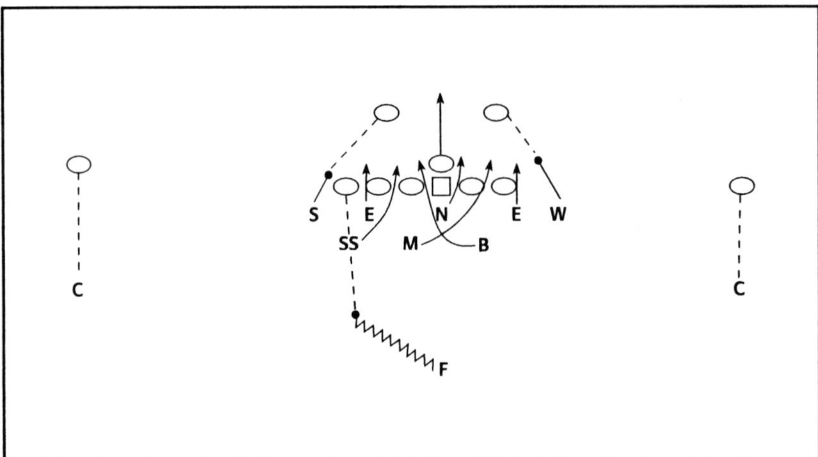

STUNT DESCRIPTION: This strong-safety blitz is an **illusion** stunt that gives the offense the illusion of an eight-man pass rush.

SECONDARY COVERAGE: Zero coverage. Stud and Whip spy the near backs, and the strong safety covers the tight end. Possible variation: The two ends spy the near backs.

STRONG SAFETY: Lines up inside shade of the tight end and four to five yards deep. Blitzes through the strongside B gap at the snap.

STUD: Rushes from the outside. Contains strongside run and chases weakside run. Spies the near back versus pass.

STRONG END: Plays 5 technique versus run. Contains the quarterback versus pass.

MIKE: Blitzes through the weakside B gap. Mike goes first. His first step is directly at his aiming point.

NOSE: Slants to the weakside A gap.

BUCK: Blitzes through the strongside A gap. Mike goes first. Buck's first step should be parallel to the line with his right foot.

WEAK END: Plays 5 technique versus run. Contains the quarterback versus pass.

WHIP: Rushes from the outside. Contains strongside run and chases weakside run. Spies the near back versus pass.

FREE SAFETY: Disguises his assignment as though he's playing cover 1. As the quarterback calls cadence, the free safety creeps to a position that enables him to cover the tight end.

STRONG CORNER: Covers receiver #1 (inside technique).

WEAK CORNER: Covers receiver #1 (inside technique).

STUNT #7

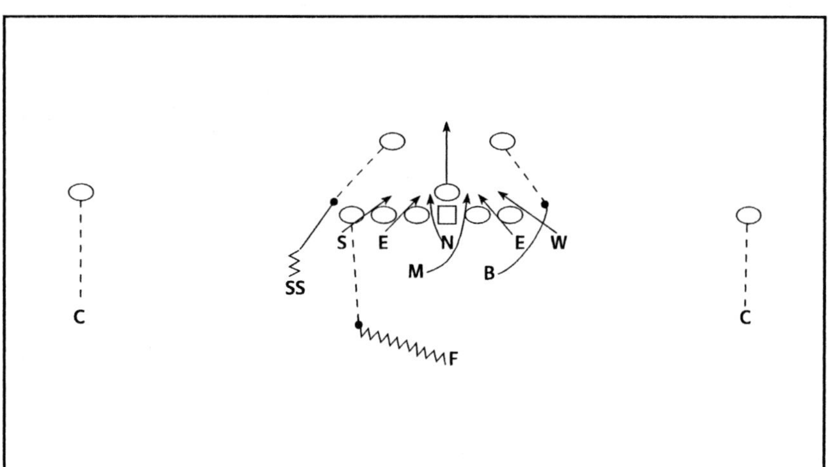

STUNT DESCRIPTION: This fake strong-safety blitz is an **illusion** stunt that gives the offense the illusion of an eight-man pass rush.

SECONDARY COVERAGE: Zero coverage. Buck and the strong safety spy the near backs, and the strong safety covers the tight end. Possible variation: Stud and Whip spy the near backs.

STRONG SAFETY: Creeps toward the line during cadence. Rushes hard from the outside at the snap. Contains strongside run and chases weakside run. Spies the near back versus pass.

STUD: Slants across the tight end's face, secures the C gap, and contains the quarterback.

STRONG END: Slants into the B gap.

MIKE: Blitzes through the weakside A gap.

NOSE: Slants to the strongside A gap.

BUCK: Stunts to the weakside D gap. Contains weakside run and spies the near back.

WEAK END: Slants into and controls the B gap.

WHIP: Rushes through the outside shoulder of the offensive tackle. Secures the C gap and contains the quarterback.

FREE SAFETY: Disguises his assignment as though he's playing cover 1. As the quarterback calls cadence, the free safety creeps to a position that enables him to cover the tight end.

STRONG CORNER: Covers receiver #1 (inside technique).

WEAK CORNER: Covers receiver #1 (inside technique).

STUNT #8

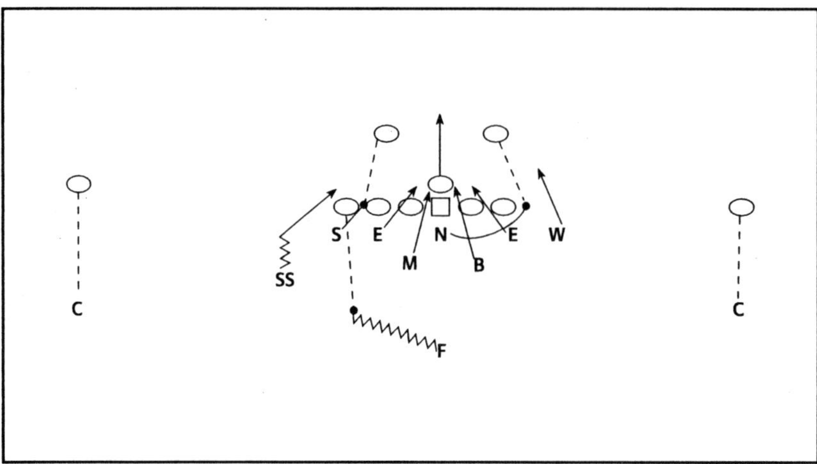

STUNT DESCRIPTION: This strong-safety blitz is an **illusion** stunt that gives the offense the illusion of an eight-man pass rush.

SECONDARY COVERAGE: Zero coverage. Stud and nose spy the near backs, and the free safety covers the tight end. Possible variation: the strong safety and Whip spy the near backs.

STRONG SAFETY: Creeps toward the line during cadence. Rushes hard from the outside at the snap. Contains pass and strongside run. Chases weakside run.

STUD: Slants across the tight end's face and secures the C gap. Spies the near back versus pass.

STRONG END: Slants into the B gap.

MIKE: Blitzes through the strongside A gap.

NOSE: Loops to the outside shoulder of the weakside offensive tackle. Secures the C gap and spies the near back.

BUCK: Blitzes through the weakside A gap.

WEAK END: Slants into and controls the B gap.

WHIP: Rushes hard from the outside. Contains pass and weakside run. Chases strongside run.

FREE SAFETY: Disguises his assignment as though he's playing cover 1. As the quarterback calls cadence, the free safety creeps to a position that enables him to cover the tight end.

STRONG CORNER: Covers receiver #1 (inside technique).

WEAK CORNER: Covers receiver #1 (inside technique).

STUNT #9

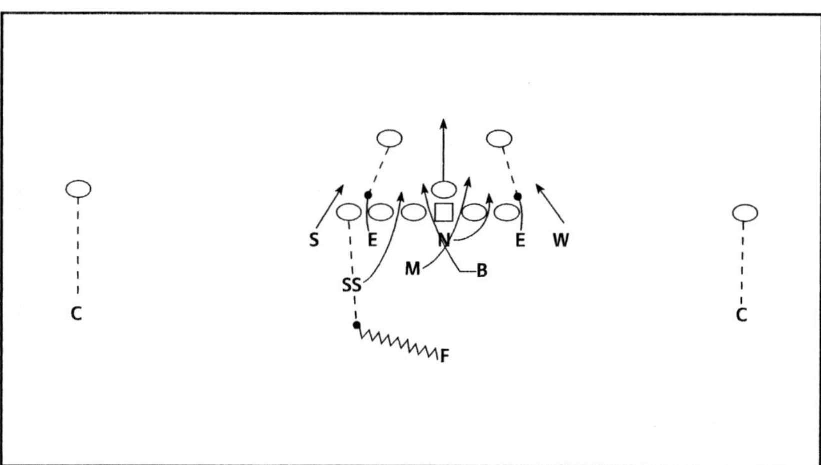

STUNT DESCRIPTION: This strong-safety blitz is an **illusion** stunt that gives the offense the illusion of an eight-man pass rush.

SECONDARY COVERAGE: Zero coverage. The two ends spy the near backs, and the free safety covers the tight end. Possible variation: Stud and Whip spy the near backs.

STRONG SAFETY: Lines up inside shade on the tight end four to five yards deep. Blitzes through the B gap at the snap of the ball.

STUD: Lines up in an 8 technique. Rushes hard from the outside. Contains the quarterback and strongside run. Chases weakside run.

STRONG END: Slants into and secures the C gap. Spies the near back.

MIKE: Blitzes through the weakside A gap. Mike goes first. His first step should be directly at his aiming point.

NOSE: Loops to the outside shoulder of the weakside guard and secures the B gap.

BUCK: Blitzes through the strongside A gap. Buck must allow Mike to go first. Buck's first step is parallel to the line with his left foot.

WEAK END: Plays 5 technique. Spies the near back versus pass.

WHIP: Rushes hard from the outside. Contains pass and weakside run. Chases strongside run.

FREE SAFETY: Disguises his assignment as though he's playing cover 1. As the quarterback calls cadence, the free safety creeps to a position that enables him to cover the tight end.

STRONG CORNER: Covers receiver #1 (inside technique).

WEAK CORNER: Covers receiver #1 (inside technique).

STUNT #10

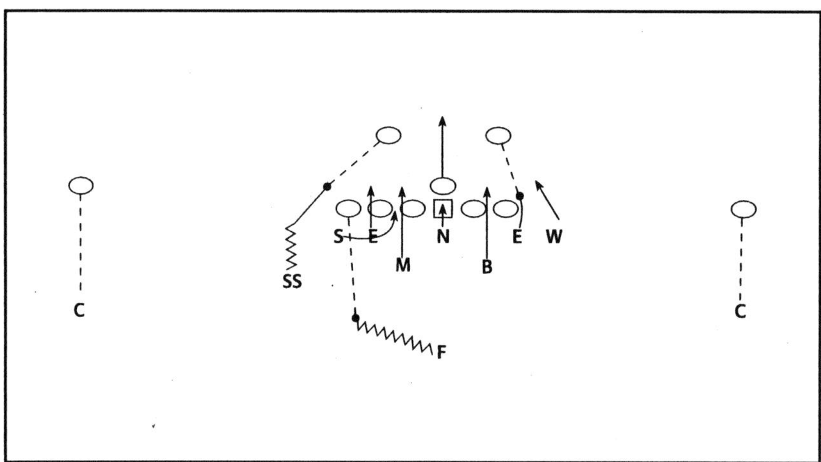

STUNT DESCRIPTION: This strong-safety blitz is an **illusion** stunt that gives the offense the illusion of an eight-man pass rush. Since Stud and Mike are both rushing through the B gap, this is also a twin stunt.

SECONDARY COVERAGE: Zero coverage. Strong safety and weakside end spy the near backs, and the free safety covers the tight end. Possible variation: both ends spy the near backs.

STRONG SAFETY: Creeps toward the line during cadence and rushes hard from the outside. Contains the quarterback and strongside run. Chases weakside run. Spies the near back versus pass.

STUD: Loops into the B gap at the snap.

STRONG END: Plays 5 technique.

MIKE: Blitzes through the outside shoulder of the offensive guard.

NOSE: Plays 0 technique.

BUCK: Blitzes through the outside shoulder of the offensive guard and secures the B gap.

WEAK END: Plays 5 technique. Spies the near back versus pass.

WHIP: Rushes hard from the outside. Contains the quarterback and weakside run. Chases strongside run.

FREE SAFETY: Disguises his assignment as though he's playing cover 1. As the quarterback calls cadence, the free safety creeps to a position that enables him to cover the tight end.

STRONG CORNER: Covers receiver #1 (inside technique).

WEAK CORNER: Covers receiver #1 (inside technique).

STUNT #11

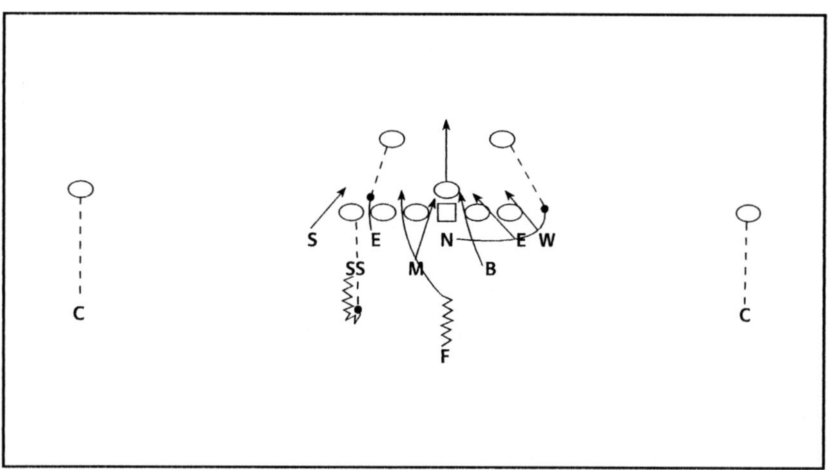

STUNT DESCRIPTION: This free-safety blitz is an **illusion** stunt that gives the offense the illusion of an eight-man pass rush.

SECONDARY COVERAGE: Zero coverage. The strong end and the nose spy the near backs, and the strong safety covers the tight end. Possible variation: Stud and Whip spy the near backs.

STRONG SAFETY: Lines up inside shade on the tight end and four to five yards deep. As the quarterback calls cadence, the strong safety slowly moves back to a position six to seven yards deep, and covers the tight end.

STUD: Lines up in an 8 technique. Rushes from the outside. Contains the quarterback and strongside run. Chases weakside run.

STRONG END: Plays 5 technique. Spies the near back.

MIKE: Blitzes through the strongside A gap.

NOSE: Loops to the outside shoulder of the weakside offensive tackle, secures the D gap, and spies the near back.

BUCK: Blitzes through the weakside A gap.

WEAK END: Slants across the offensive tackle's face into the B gap.

WHIP: Charges through the outside shoulder of the offensive tackle and secures the C gap.

FREE SAFETY: Disguises his assignment as though he's playing cover 1. As the quarterback calls cadence, the free safety creeps toward the line and blitzes through the strongside B gap.

STRONG CORNER: Covers receiver #1 (inside technique).

WEAK CORNER: Covers receiver #1 (inside technique).

STUNT #12

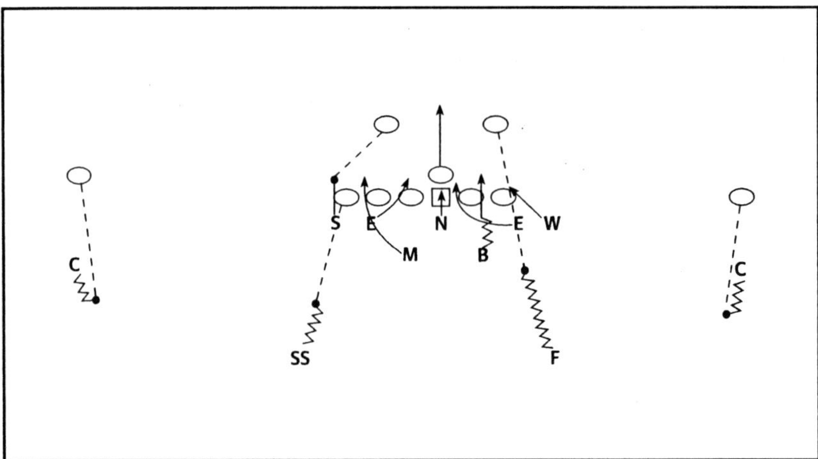

STUNT DESCRIPTION: This fake free-safety blitz is an **illusion** stunt that gives the offense the illusion of a seven-man pass rush.

SECONDARY COVERAGE: Zero coverage disguised as cover 2. Stud and the free safety spy the near backs, and the strong safety covers the tight end. Possible variation: Mike and the free safety spy the near backs.

STRONG SAFETY: Disguises his assignment from a cover 2 look. As the quarterback calls cadence, the strong safety moves to a position that enables him to cover the tight end.

STUD: Plays 9 technique. Spies the near back.

STRONG END: Slants into and controls the B gap.

MIKE: Blitzes through the strongside C gap.

NOSE: Plays 0 technique.

BUCK: Creeps toward the line during cadence and attacks the offensive guard's outside shoulder as the ball is being snapped.

WEAK END: Loops into the weakside A gap at the snap of the ball.

WHIP: Charges through the outside shoulder of the offensive tackle and secures the C gap.

FREE SAFETY: Disguises his assignment as though he's playing cover 2. As the quarterback calls cadence, the free safety creeps toward the line and gives the quarterback the a impression that a weakside blitz is in progress. Contains weakside run and covers the near back versus pass.

STRONG CORNER: Covers receiver #1 (inside technique from a cover 2 disguise).

WEAK CORNER: Covers receiver #1 (inside technique from a cover 2 disguise).

STUNT #13

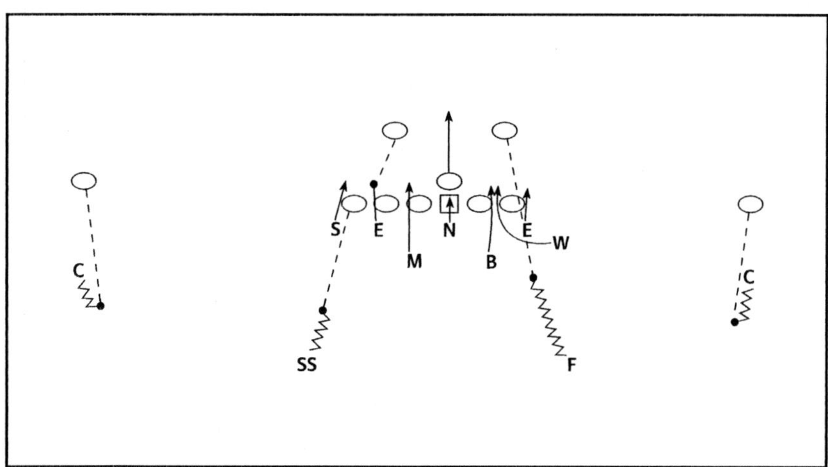

STUNT DESCRIPTION: This fake free-safety blitz is an **illusion** stunt that gives the offense the illusion of a seven-man pass rush. Since Buck and Whip are both stunting through the same gap, this is also a twin stunt.

SECONDARY COVERAGE: Zero coverage disguised as cover 2. The strong end and the free safety spy the near backs, and the strong safety covers the tight end. Possible variation: Stud and the free safety spy the near backs.

STRONG SAFETY: Disguises his assignment from a cover 2 look. As the quarterback calls cadence, the strong safety moves to a position that enables him to cover the tight end.

STUD: Plays 9 technique versus run. Contains the quarterback versus pass.

STRONG END: Plays 5 technique. Spies the near back.

MIKE: Blitzes through the outside shoulder of the offensive guard and secures the B gap.

NOSE: Plays 0 technique.

BUCK: Blitzes through the offensive guard's outside shoulder at the snap.

WEAK END: Plays 5 technique.

WHIP: Loops into the weakside B gap at the snap of the ball.

FREE SAFETY: Disguises his assignment as though he's playing cover 2. As the quarterback calls cadence, the free safety creeps toward the line and gives the quarterback the impression that a weakside blitz is in progress. Contains weakside run and covers the near back versus pass.

STRONG CORNER: Covers receiver #1 (inside technique from a cover 2 disguise).

WEAK CORNER: Covers receiver #1 (inside technique from a cover 2 disguise).

STUNT #14

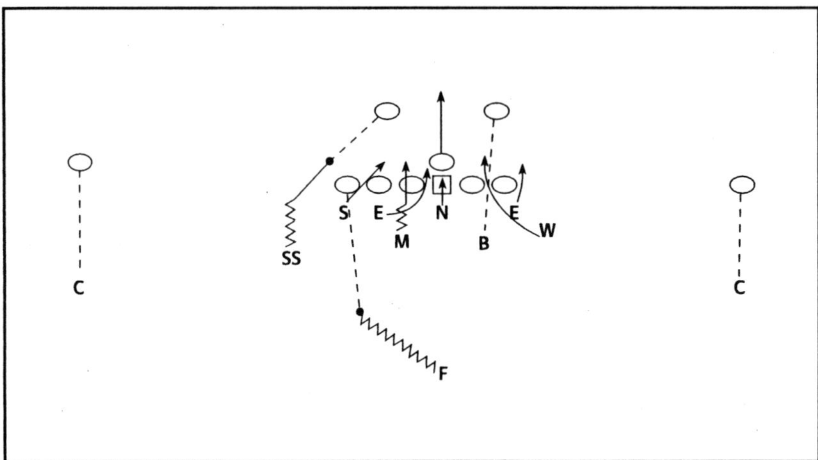

STUNT DESCRIPTION: This fake strong safety blitz is an **illusion** stunt that gives the offense the illusion of a seven-man pass rush.

SECONDARY COVERAGE: Zero coverage disguised as cover 1. The strong safety and Buck cover the two running backs, and the free safety covers the tight end. Possible variation: Stud and Buck cover the running backs.

STRONG SAFETY: Disguises his assignment from a cover 1 look. As the quarterback calls cadence, the strong safety creeps toward the line and gives the quarterback the impression that a strong safety blitz is in progress. Contains strongside run and chases weakside run. Spies the near back versus pass.

STUD: Slants across the tight end's face into the C gap. Secures the C gap and contains the quarterback.

STRONG END: Loops into the A gap at the snap.

MIKE: Creeps toward the line and attacks the offensive guard's outside shoulder as the ball is being snapped.

NOSE: Plays 0 technique.

BUCK: Scrapes outside and contains versus weakside run. Shuffles down the line and checks counter and cutback versus strongside run. Covers the near back versus pass.

WEAK END: Plays 5 technique.

WHIP: Loops into the weakside B gap at the snap of the ball.

FREE SAFETY: Disguises his assignment as though he's playing cover 1. As the quarterback calls cadence, the free safety moves to a position that enables him to cover the tight end.

STRONG CORNER: Covers receiver #1 (inside technique).

WEAK CORNER: Covers receiver #1 (inside technique).

STUNT #15

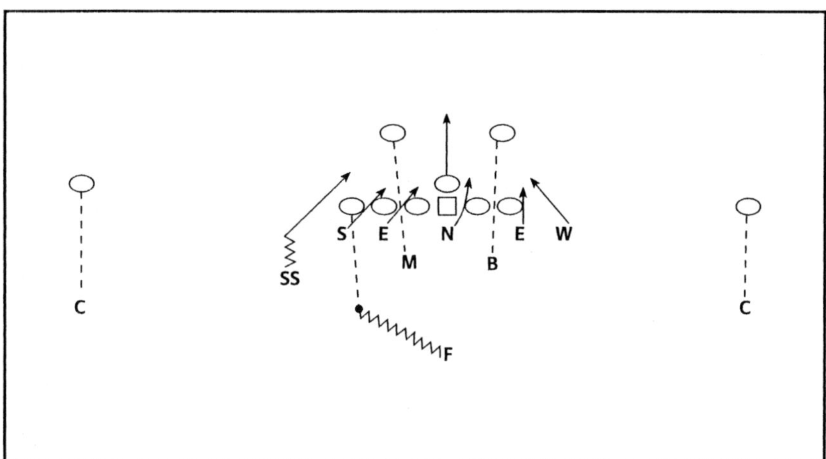

STUNT DESCRIPTION: This strong safety blitz gives the defense a six-man pass rush.

SECONDARY COVERAGE: Zero coverage disguised as cover 1. Mike and Buck cover the two running backs, and the free safety covers the tight end.

STRONG SAFETY: Disguises his assignment from a cover 1 look. As the quarterback calls cadence, the strong safety moves toward the line and rushes hard from the outside. Contains the quarterback and strongside run. Chases weakside run.

STUD: Slants across the tight end's face into the C gap.

STRONG END: Slants across the offensive tackle's face into the B gap.

MIKE: Mike has no gap responsibility versus run. Pursues strongside and weakside run from an inside-out position. Covers the near back versus pass.

NOSE: Slants into the weakside A gap at the snap.

BUCK: Plugs the B gap versus weakside run. Checks the strong A gap and then shuffles down the line looking for counter and cutback versus strongside run. Covers the near back versus pass.

WEAK END: Plays 5 technique.

WHIP: Rushes hard from the outside. Contains the quarterback and weakside run. Chases strongside run.

FREE SAFETY: Disguises his assignment as though he's playing cover 1. As the quarterback calls cadence, the free safety moves to a position that enables him to cover the tight end.

STRONG CORNER: Covers receiver #1 (inside technique).

WEAK CORNER: Covers receiver #1 (inside technique).

STUNT #16

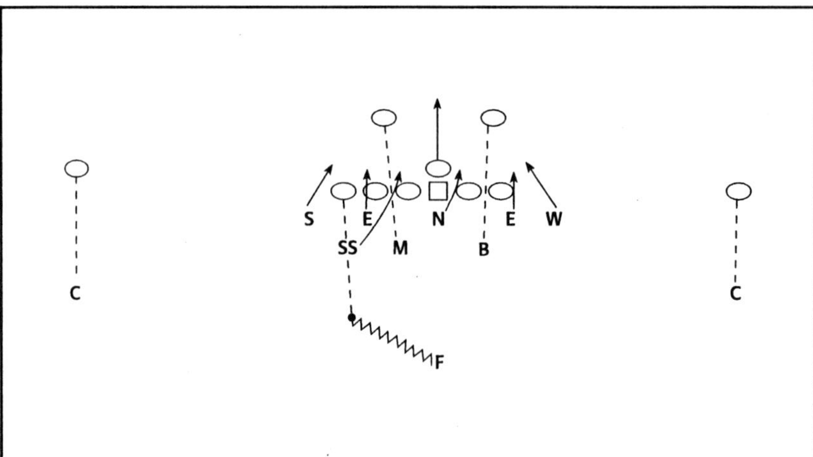

STUNT DESCRIPTION: This strong safety blitz gives the defense a six-man pass rush.

SECONDARY COVERAGE: Zero coverage disguised as cover 1. Mike and Buck cover the two running backs, and the free safety covers the tight end.

STRONG SAFETY: Lines up inside shade on the tight end and four to five yards deep. At the snap, he blitzes through the B gap.

STUD: Lines up in a loose 8 technique and rushes hard off the edge. Contains the quarterback and strongside run. Chases weakside run.

STRONG END: Plays 5 technique.

MIKE: Mike has no gap responsibility. Pursues strongside and weakside run from an inside-out position. Covers the near back versus pass.

NOSE: Slants into the weakside A gap.

BUCK: Secures the B gap versus weakside run. Secures the strong A gap and then shuffles down the line checking for counter and cutback versus strongside run. Covers the near back versus pass.

WEAK END: Plays 5 technique.

WHIP: Rushes hard from the outside. Contains the quarterback and weakside run. Chases strongside run.

FREE SAFETY: Disguises his assignment as though he's playing cover 1. As the quarterback calls cadence, the free safety moves to a position that enables him to cover the tight end.

STRONG CORNER: Covers receiver #1(inside technique).

WEAK CORNER: Covers receiver #1(inside technique).

STUNT #17

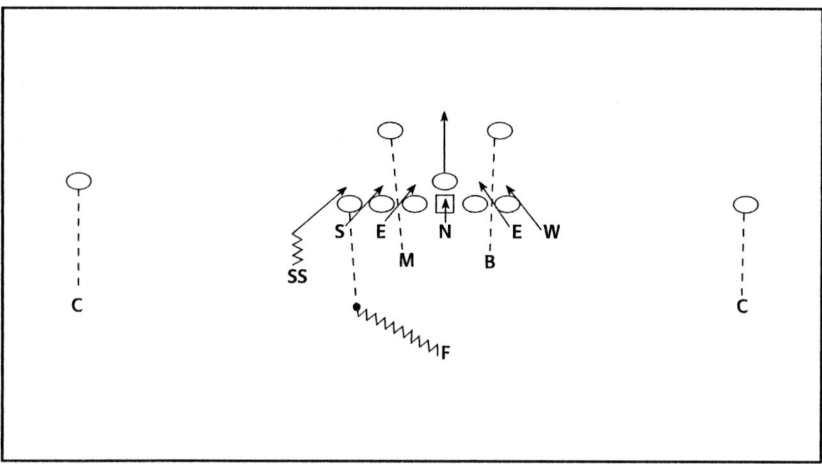

STUNT DESCRIPTION: This strong safety blitz gives the defense a six-man pass rush.

SECONDARY COVERAGE: Zero coverage disguised as cover 1. Mike and Buck cover the two running backs, and the free safety covers the tight end.

STRONG SAFETY: Moves toward the line during cadence and rushes from the edge at the snap. Contains the quarterback and strongside run. Chases weakside run.

STUD: Slants across the tight end's face and secures the C gap.

STRONG END: Slants across the tackle's face and controls the B gap.

MIKE: Mike has no gap responsibility. Pursues strongside and weakside run from an inside-out position. Covers the near back versus pass.

NOSE: Plays 0 technique

BUCK: Scrapes outside and contains the play versus weakside run. Pursues from an inside-out position, checking for counter and cutback versus strongside run. Covers the near back versus pass.

WEAK END: Slants across the tackle's face and secures the B gap.

WHIP: Charges through the outside shoulder of the offensive tackle and controls the C gap.

FREE SAFETY: Disguises his assignment as though he's playing cover 1. As the quarterback calls cadence, the free safety moves to a position that enables him to cover the tight end.

STRONG CORNER: Covers receiver #1 (inside technique).

WEAK CORNER: Covers receiver #1 (inside technique).

STUNT #18

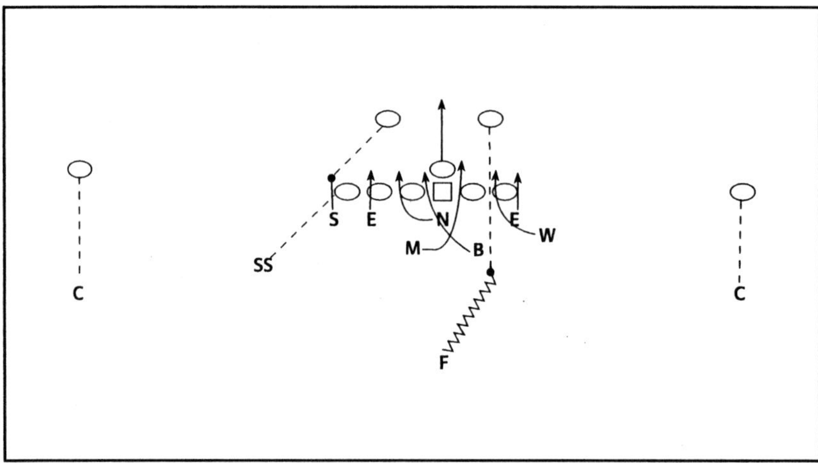

STUNT DESCRIPTION: This fake free safety blitz gives the **illusion** of a seven-man pass rush.

SECONDARY COVERAGE: Zero coverage disguised as cover 1. Stud and the free safety cover the two running backs, and the strong safety covers the tight end.

STRONG SAFETY: Covers the tight end.

STUD: Plays 9 technique versus run. Spies the near back versus pass.

STRONG END: Plays 5 technique versus run. Contains quarterback versus pass.

MIKE: Blitzes through the weakside A gap. Makes his first step parallel to the line with his right foot to allow Buck to go first.

NOSE: Loops across the offensive guard's face into the strongside B gap.

BUCK: Blitzes through the strongside A gap. Buck goes first.

WEAK END: Plays 5 technique versus run. Contains the quarterback versus pass.

WHIP: Blitzes through the weakside B gap.

FREE SAFETY: Disguises his assignment as though he's playing cover 1. As the quarterback calls cadence, the free safety moves toward the line and fakes a weakside blitz. Contains weakside run and covers the near back versus pass.

STRONG CORNER: Covers receiver #1 (inside technique).

WEAK CORNER: Covers receiver #1 (inside technique).

STUNT #19

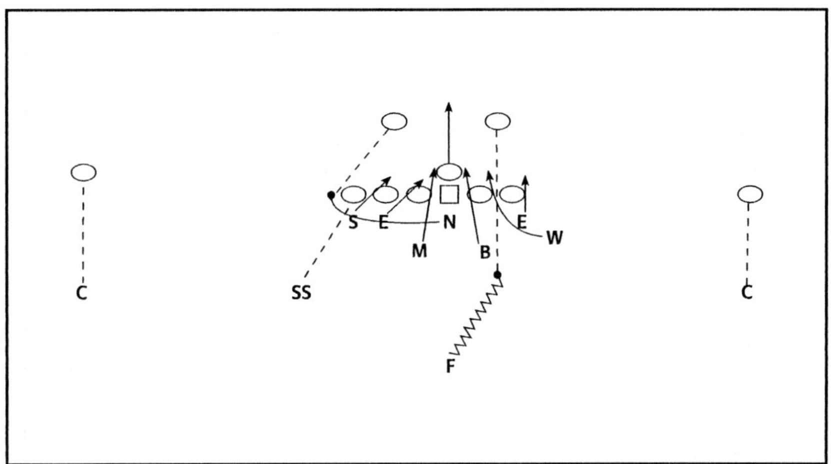

STUNT DESCRIPTION: This fake free safety blitz gives the **illusion** of a seven-man pass rush.

SECONDARY COVERAGE: Zero coverage disguised as cover 1. The nose and free safety cover the two running backs, and the strong safety covers the tight end.

STRONG SAFETY: Covers the tight end.

STUD: Slants across the tight end's face into the C gap. Secures the C gap and contains the quarterback.

STRONG END: Slants across the offensive tackle's face into the B gap.

MIKE: Blitzes through the strongside A gap.

NOSE: Loops across the tight end's face into the D gap. Contains strongside run and chases weakside run. Spies the near back versus pass.

BUCK: Blitzes through the weakside A gap.

WEAK END: Plays 5 technique versus run. Contains the quarterback versus pass.

WHIP: Blitzes through the weakside B gap.

FREE SAFETY: Disguises his assignment as though he's playing cover 1. As the quarterback calls cadence, the free safety moves toward the line and fakes a weakside blitz. Contains weakside run and covers the near back versus pass.

STRONG CORNER: Covers receiver #1 (inside technique).

WEAK CORNER: Covers receiver #1 (inside technique).

STUNT #20

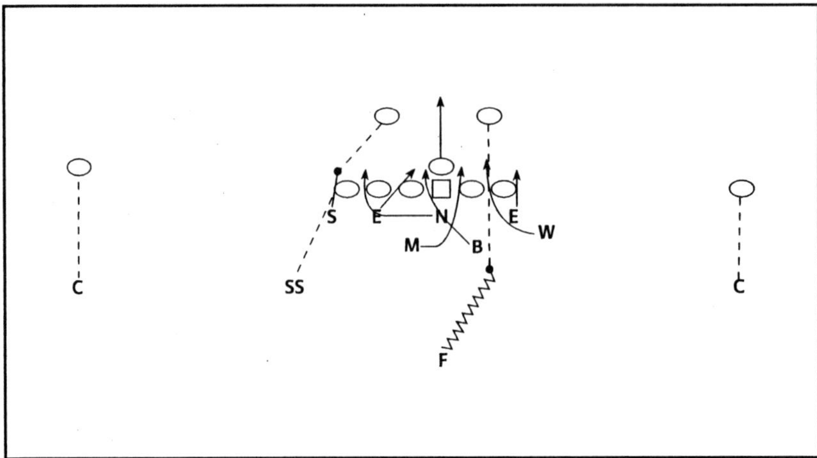

STUNT DESCRIPTION: This fake free safety blitz gives the **illusion** of a seven-man pass rush.

SECONDARY COVERAGE: Zero coverage disguised as cover 1. Stud and the free safety cover the two running backs, and the strong safety covers the tight end.

STRONG SAFETY: Covers the tight end.

STUD: Plays 9 technique versus run. Spies the near back versus pass.

STRONG END: Slants across the offensive tackle's face into the B gap.

MIKE: Blitzes through the weakside A gap. Mike makes his first step parallel to the line with his right foot to allow Buck to go first.

NOSE: Loops across the offensive tackle's face into the C gap. Secures the C gap and contains the quarterback.

BUCK: Blitzes through the strongside A gap. Buck goes first, taking his first step directly at his aiming point.

WEAK END: Plays 5 technique versus run. Contains the quarterback versus pass.

WHIP: Blitzes through the weakside B gap.

FREE SAFETY: Disguises his assignment as though he's playing cover 1. As the quarterback calls cadence, the free safety moves toward the line and fakes a weakside blitz. Contains weakside run and covers the near back versus pass.

STRONG CORNER: Covers receiver #1 (inside technique).

WEAK CORNER: Covers receiver #1 (inside technique).

STUNT #21

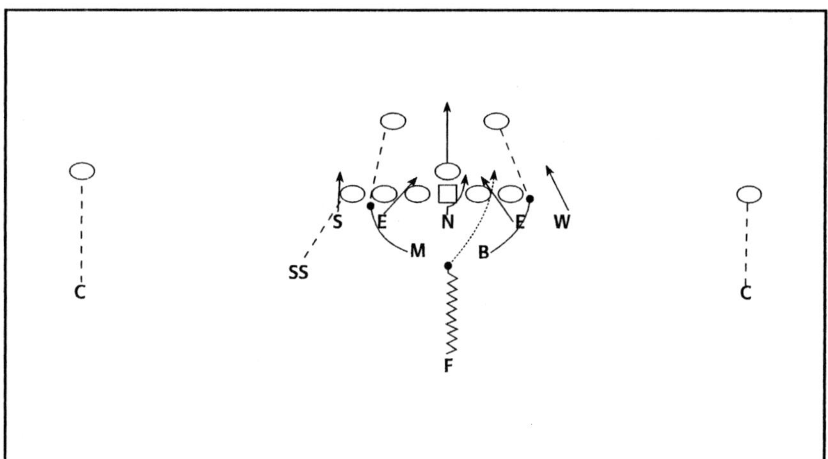

STUNT DESCRIPTION: This delayed free safety blitz gives the **illusion** of an eight-man pass rush and provides the defense with a weakside overload.

SECONDARY COVERAGE: Zero coverage disguised as cover 1. Mike and Buck spy the two running backs, and the strong safety covers the tight end.

STRONG SAFETY: Covers the tight end.

STUD: Plays 9 technique versus run. Contains the quarterback versus pass.

STRONG END: Slants across the offensive tackle's face into the B gap.

MIKE: Fakes a blitz into the C gap. Secures the C gap and spies the near back.

NOSE: Plays 0 technique versus run. Rushes hard through the weakside A gap versus pass.

BUCK: Fakes a blitz into the C gap. Secures the C gap and spies the near back.

WEAK END: Slants across the offensive tackle's face into the B gap

WHIP: Rushes hard from the edge. Contains the quarterback and weakside run. Chases strongside run.

FREE SAFETY: Disguises his assignment as though he's playing cover 1. As the quarterback calls cadence, the free safety moves toward the line. He should be directly behind the nose and about five yards deep as the ball is snapped. He is the cutback defender versus run. Delay-blitzes through the weakside B gap versus pass.

STRONG CORNER: Covers receiver #1 (inside technique).

WEAK CORNER: Covers receiver #1 (inside technique).

STUNT #22

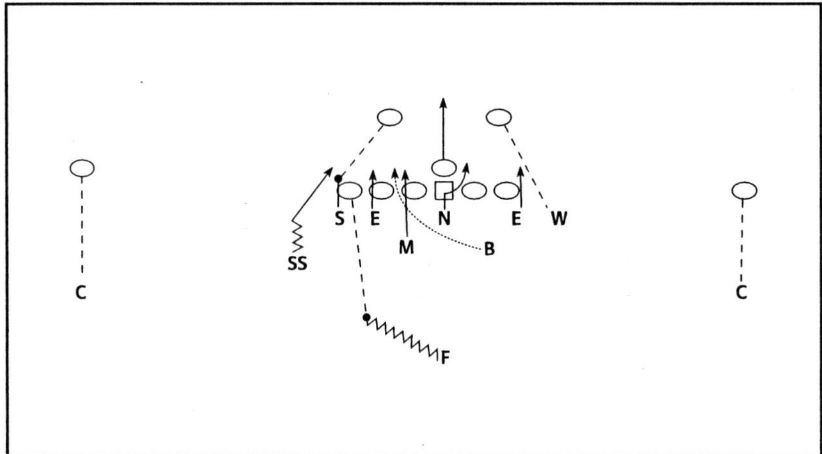

STUNT DESCRIPTION: This strong safety blitz gives the defense a strongside overload.

SECONDARY COVERAGE: Zero coverage disguised as cover 1. Stud and Whip cover the two running backs, and the free safety covers the tight end.

STRONG SAFETY: Moves toward the line during cadence and rushes from the edge. Contains the quarterback and strongside run. Chases weakside run.

STUD: Plays 9 technique versus run. Spies the near back versus pass.

STRONG END: Plays 5 technique.

MIKE: Blitzes through the outside shoulder of the offensive guard.

NOSE: Plays 0 technique versus run. Rushes through the weakside A gap versus pass.

BUCK: Plays base technique versus run. Delay rushes through the strongside B gap versus pass.

WEAK END: Plays 5 technique versus run. Contains the quarterback versus pass.

WHIP: Plays 9 technique versus run. Covers the near back versus pass.

FREE SAFETY: Disguises his assignment as though he's playing cover 1. As the quarterback calls cadence, the free safety moves to a position that enables him to cover the tight end.

STRONG CORNER: Covers receiver #1 (inside technique).

WEAK CORNER: Covers receiver #1 (inside technique).

STUNT #23

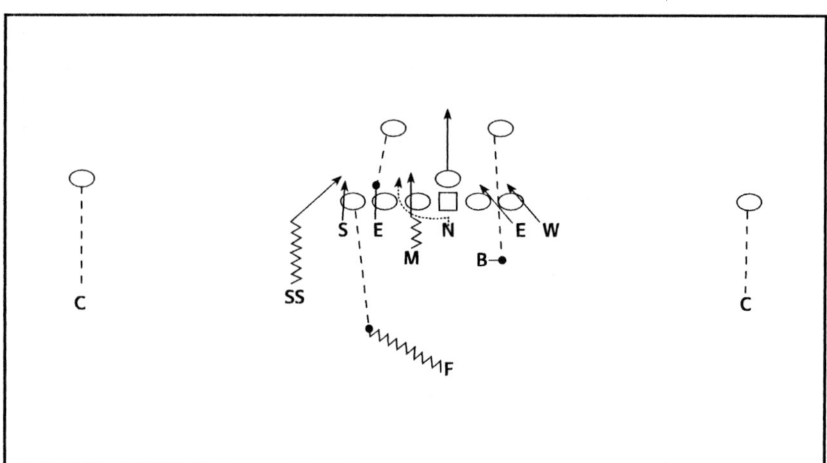

STUNT DESCRIPTION: This strong safety blitz gives the defense a strongside overload.

SECONDARY COVERAGE: Zero coverage disguised as cover 1. The strong end and Buck cover the two running backs, and the free safety covers the tight end.

STRONG SAFETY: Moves toward the line during cadence and rushes from the edge. Contains the quarterback and strongside run. Chases weakside run.

STUD: Plays 9 technique.

STRONG END: Plays 5 technique versus run. Spies the near back versus pass.

MIKE: Creeps toward the line during cadence and blitzes through the outside shoulder of the offensive guard.

NOSE: Plays 0 technique versus run. Delay rushes through the strongside B gap versus pass.

BUCK: Shuffles slightly to his outside at the snap. Scrapes outside and contains versus weakside run. Covers the near back versus pass.

WEAK END: Slants across the offensive tackle's face into the B gap.

WHIP: Rushes through the outside shoulder of the offensive tackle. Secures the C gap and contains the quarterback.

FREE SAFETY: Disguises his assignment as though he's playing cover 1. As the quarterback calls cadence, the free safety moves to a position that enables him to cover the tight end.

STRONG CORNER: Covers receiver #1 (inside technique).

WEAK CORNER: Covers receiver #1 (inside technique).

STUNT #24

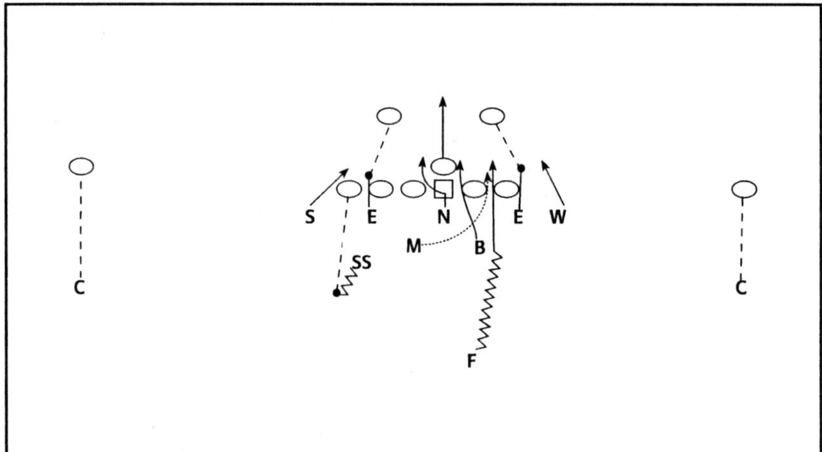

STUNT DESCRIPTION: This delayed linebacker/free safety blitz gives the **illusion** of an eight-man pass rush and provides the defense with a weakside overload.

SECONDARY COVERAGE: Zero coverage disguised as cover 1. Both ends spy the two running backs, and the strong safety covers the tight end.

STRONG SAFETY: Lines up inside shade on the tight end and four to five yards deep. Covers the tight end.

STUD: Lines up in an 8 technique and rushes hard from the edge. Contains the quarterback and strongside run. Chases weakside run.

STRONG END: Plays 5 technique versus the run. Spies the near back versus pass.

MIKE: Plays base technique versus run. Delay blitzes through the weakside B gap versus pass.

NOSE: Plays 0 technique versus run. Rushes through the strongside A gap versus pass.

BUCK: Blitzes through the weakside A gap.

WEAK END: Plays 5 technique versus the run. Spies the near back versus pass.

WHIP: Rushes hard from the edge. Contains the quarterback and weakside run. Chases strongside run.

FREE SAFETY: Disguises his assignment as though he were playing cover 1. As the quarterback calls cadence, the free safety moves toward the line and blitzes through the weakside B gap.

STRONG CORNER: Covers receiver #1 (inside technique).

WEAK CORNER: Covers receiver #1 (inside technique).

STUNT #25

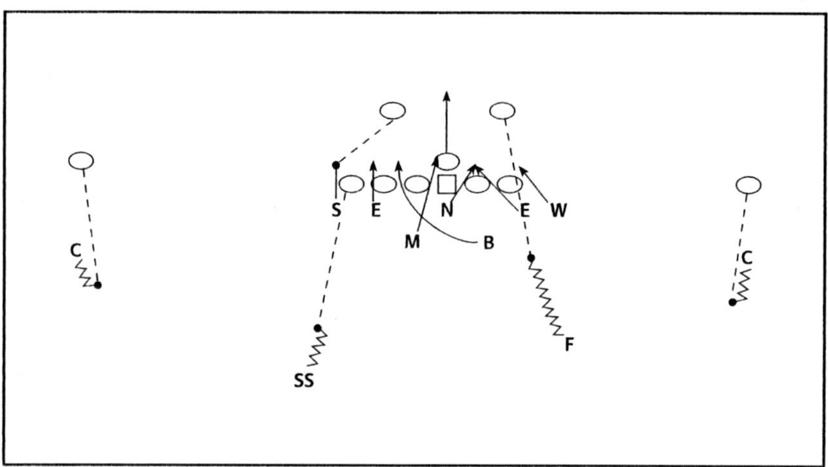

STUNT DESCRIPTION: This is an illusion stunt that gives the offense the **illusion** of a seven-man pass rush.

SECONDARY COVERAGE: Zero coverage, disguised as cover 2 with the threat of a free safety blitz. Stud and the free safety cover the near backs, and the strong safety covers the tight end.

STRONG SAFETY: Covers the tight end. Disguises his assignment as cover 2.

STUD: Plays 9 technique versus run. Spies the near back versus pass.

STRONG END: Plays 5 technique versus run. Contains the quarterback versus pass.

MIKE: Blitzes through the strongside A gap.

NOSE: Slants into the weakside A gap.

BUCK: Blitzes through the strongside B gap.

WEAK END: Slants across the offensive tackle's face into the B gap.

WHIP: Rushes through the outside shoulder of the offensive tackle. Secures the C gap and contains the quarterback.

FREE SAFETY: Disguises his assignment as though he's playing cover 2. As the quarterback calls cadence, the free safety moves toward the line as though he intends to blitz. As the ball is snapped, he is in position to cover the near back and contain weakside run.

STRONG CORNER: Covers receiver #1 (inside technique disguised as cover 2 man).

WEAK CORNER: Covers receiver #1 (inside technique disguised as cover 2 man).

STUNT #26

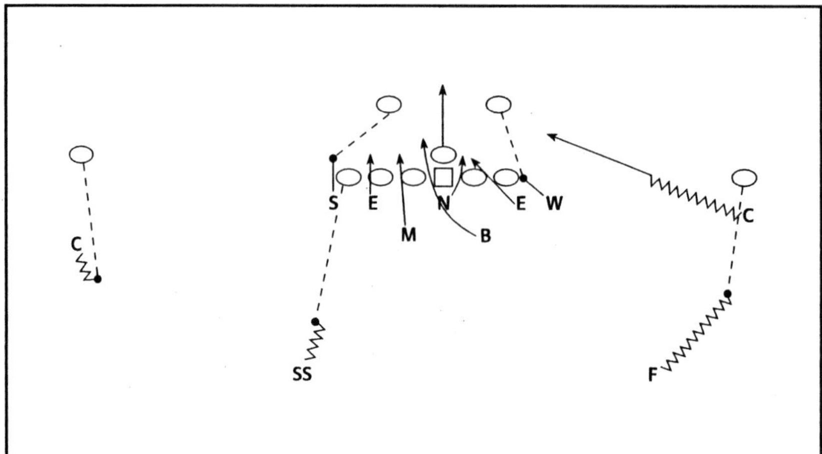

STUNT DESCRIPTION: This weak cornerback blitz is an illusion stunt that gives the offense the **illusion** of an eight-man pass rush.

SECONDARY COVERAGE: Zero coverage. Stud and Whip spy the near backs, and the strong safety covers the tight end.

STRONG SAFETY: Disguises his coverage as cover 2. As the quarterback calls cadence, the strong safety slowly creeps to a position that enables him to cover the tight end.

STUD: Plays 9 technique versus run. Spies the near back versus pass.

STRONG END: Plays 5 technique.

MIKE: Blitzes through the outside shoulder of the offensive guard and secures the B gap.

NOSE: Slants into the weakside A gap.

BUCK: Blitzes through the strongside A gap.

WEAK END: Slants across the offensive tackle's face into the B gap.

WHIP: Rushes through the outside shoulder of the offensive tackle. Secures the C gap and spies the near back.

FREE SAFETY: Disguises his assignment as though he's playing cover 2. As the quarterback calls cadence, the free safety moves to a position that enables him to cover the split end (inside technique).

STRONG CORNER: Creeps inside during cadence. He should attain full stride as the ball is being snapped. Contains the quarterback and weakside run. Chases strongside run.

WEAK CORNER: Covers receiver #1 (inside technique disguised as cover 2 man).

STUNT #27

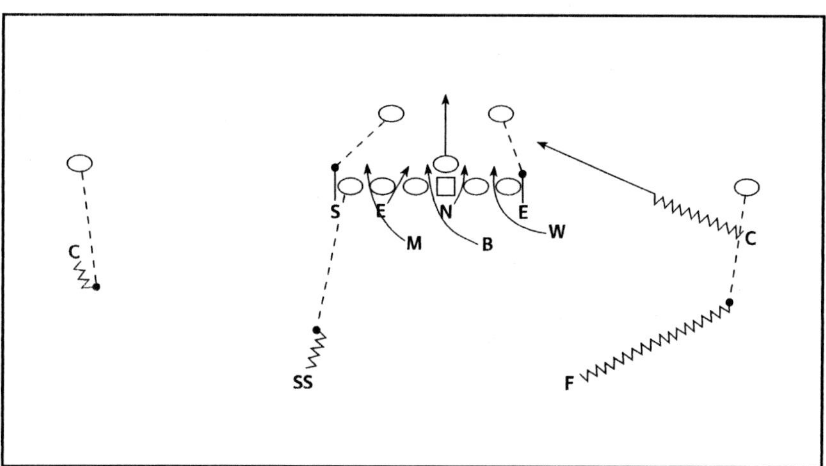

STUNT DESCRIPTION: This weak cornerback blitz is an illusion stunt that gives the offense the **illusion** of an eight-man pass rush.

SECONDARY COVERAGE: Zero coverage. Stud and the weak end spy the near backs, and the strong safety covers the tight end.

STRONG SAFETY: Disguises his coverage as cover 2. As the quarterback calls cadence, the strong safety slowly creeps to a position that enables him to cover the tight end.

STUD: Plays 9 technique versus run. Spies the near back versus pass.

STRONG END: Slants across the face of the offensive tackle into the B gap.

MIKE: Blitzes through the weakside C gap. Secures the C gap against run and contains the quarterback versus pass.

NOSE: Slants into the weakside A gap.

BUCK: Blitzes through the strongside A gap.

WEAK END: Plays 5 technique versus run. Spies the near back versus pass.

WHIP: Blitzes through the B gap.

FREE SAFETY: Disguises his assignment as though he's playing cover 2. As the quarterback calls cadence, the free safety moves to a position that enables him to cover the split end (inside technique).

STRONG CORNER: Creeps inside during cadence. He should attain full stride as the ball is being snapped. Contains the quarterback and weakside run. Chases strongside run.

WEAK CORNER: Covers receiver #1 (inside technique disguised as cover 2 man).

CHAPTER 4

COVER 1 STUNTS

Cover 1 is a man-to-man coverage with either the strong safety or the free safety free. The strength of this coverage is that there is always a safety free to key the ball, play center field, and backup the three other defensive backs and the seven defenders in the box. Another strength of this coverage is that it is a man-to-man coverage, and the offense cannot use high-low zones or attack seams. A third strength is that this coverage is easily disguised, which inhibits a quarterback's pre-snap read.

While cover 1 is not as risky as zero coverage, it also does not exert as much pressure on the offense. This weakness can be somewhat offset by incorporating the tactic of *illusion* into the stunt package. Banjo and gumbo are two very important *illusion* tactics that will be implemented in this coverage.

Banjo

As noted in Chapter 1, whenever banjo is employed, three defenders drop into three areas (**Abel**, **Baker**, and **Charlie**) and share the joint responsibility of covering the tight end and the two running backs. Each defender is responsible for covering any of the three named receivers who may enter his area. Figures 4-1a through 4-1d show how this concept functions against four common pass patterns that are frequently used to attack it. In Figures 4-1a to 4-1d, the strong safety is dropping **Abel** banjo; Mike is dropping **Baker** banjo; and Buck is dropping **Charlie** banjo.

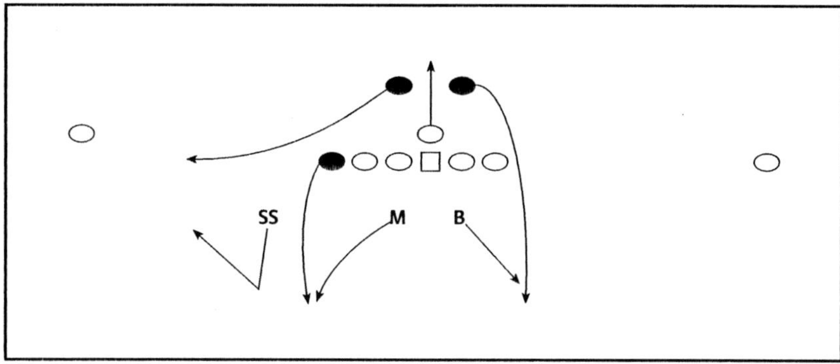

Figure 4-1a

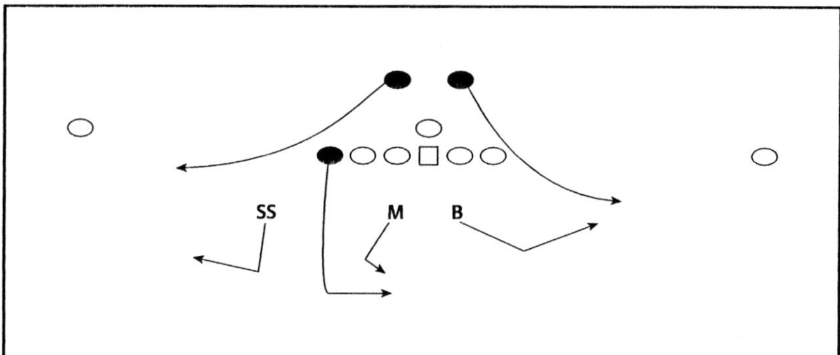

Figure 4-1b

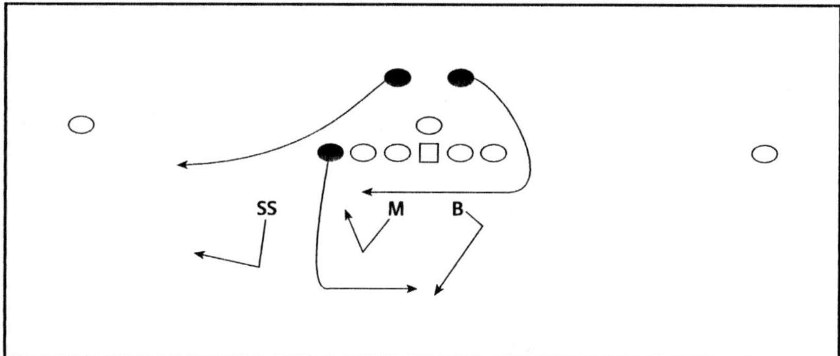

Figure 4-1c

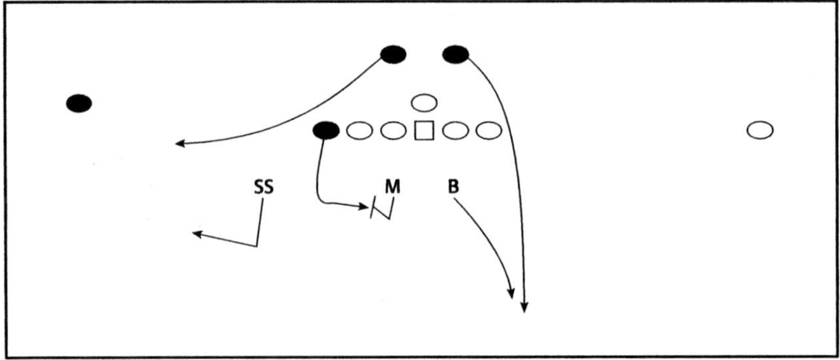

Figure 4-1d

Gumbo

Gumbo is a simpler concept for defenders to master than banjo because only two defenders are being asked to inside-out-combo cover two receivers (the tight end and strongside halfback). These two defenders do not have to concern themselves with the problems that additional crossing patterns by a third receiver can create. Figures 4-2a

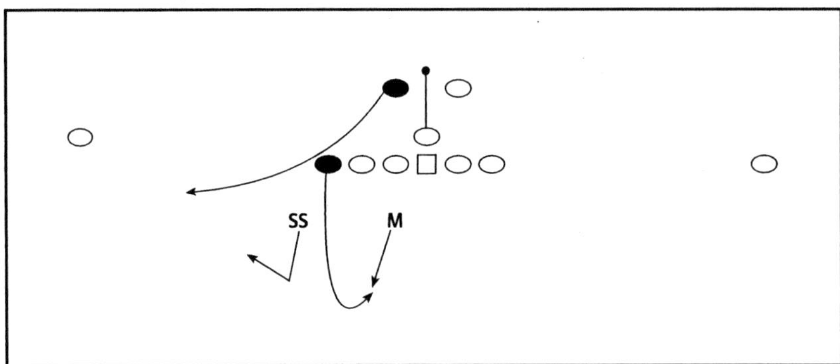

Figure 4-2a

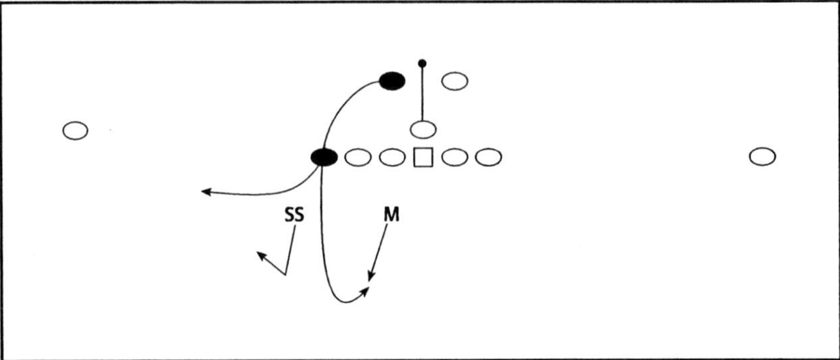

Figure 4-2b

through 4-2d illustrate how gumbo functions versus four common patterns that are frequently used to attack it. In the illustration, the strong safety is dropping **Abel** gumbo, and Mike is dropping **Baker** gumbo.

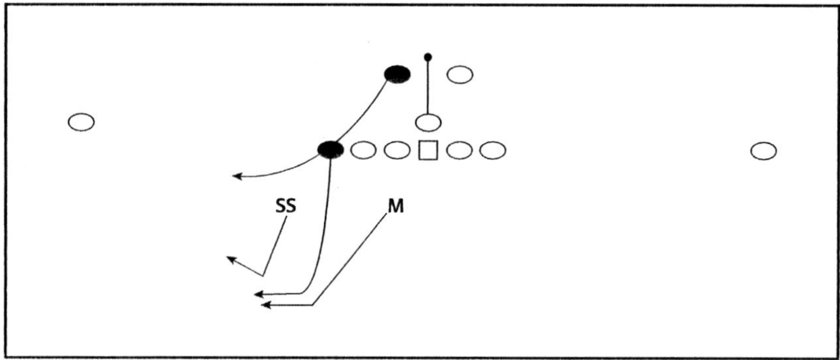

Figure 4-2c

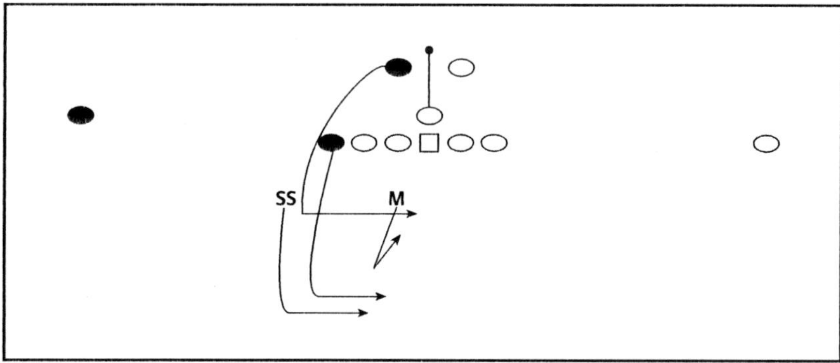

Figure 4-2d

Whom Can the Safety Help?

Although cover 1 employs a free safety, the two cornerbacks can't realistically count on the free safety to assist them with all deep patterns. The field is simply too wide to expect the free safety to cover the entire area between the two sidelines. When a cornerback can expect inside help from the free safety, he should employ an outside-leverage technique. When a cornerback can't expect inside help, he should employ an inside-leverage technique. Figure 4-3 illustrates four common formation strength/field-position situations that determine the cornerback's leverage technique.

In Figure 4-3A, the strong cornerback cannot expect to receive inside help. He should therefore maintain inside leverage on the flanker. Because both receivers in Figure 4-3B assumed tight splits, both cornerbacks can expect to receive inside help and should maintain outside leverage. Although the ball is in the middle of the field in

Figure 4-3C, both the flanker and the split end have assumed wide splits. The two cornerbacks should therefore maintain inside leverage because it is doubtful that the free safety can help either of them with inside routes. In Figure 4-3D, the weak cornerback can expect to receive inside help from the free safety. He should, therefore, employ an outside-leverage technique.

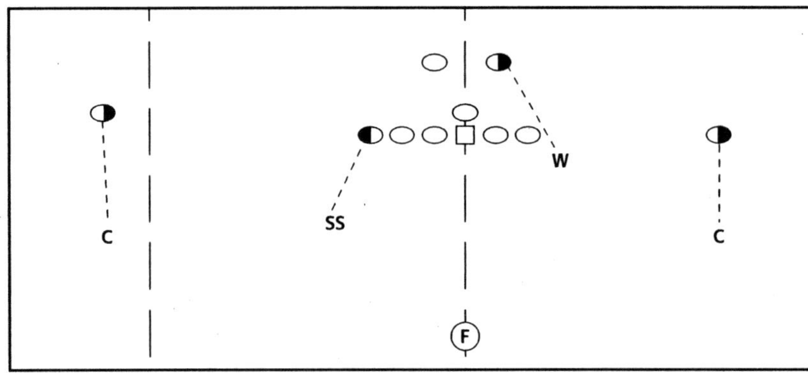

Figure 4-3a

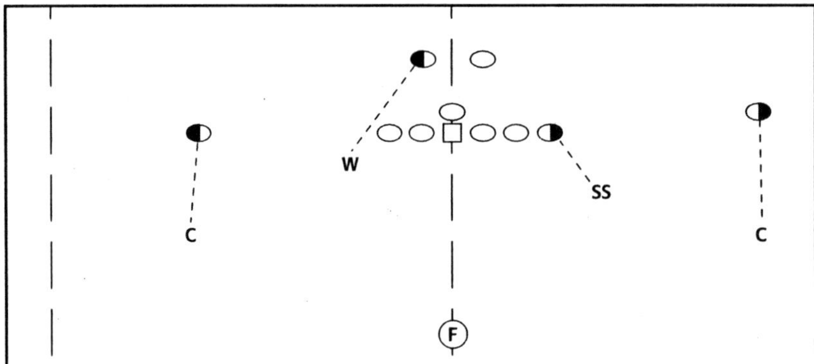

Figure 4-3b

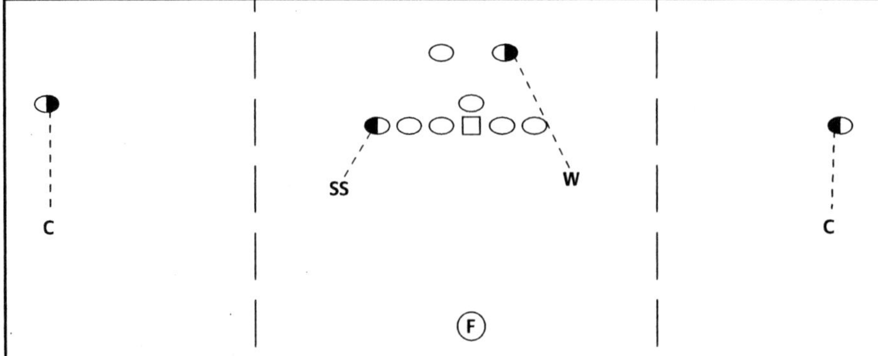

Figure 4-3c

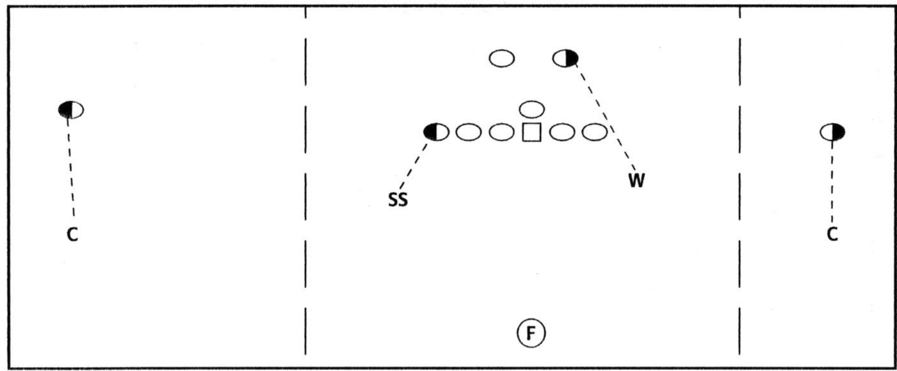

Figure 4-3d

STUNT #28

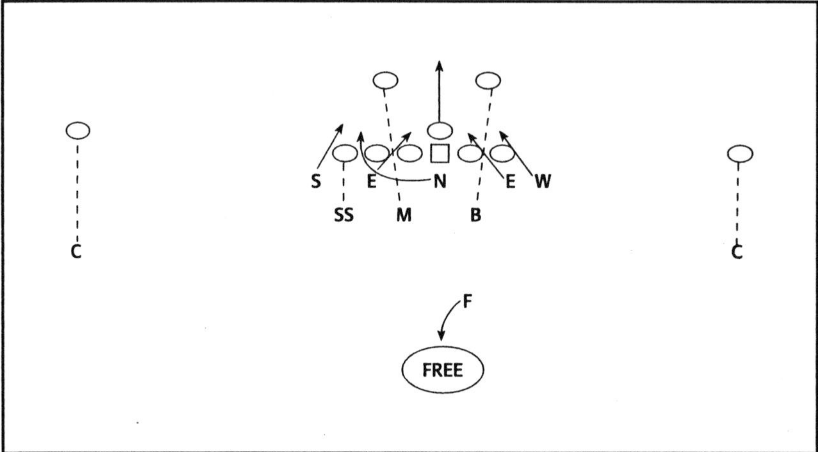

STUNT DESCRIPTION: This is a simple dog that has both outside linebackers rushing hard off the edge.

SECONDARY COVERAGE: Cover 1. Mike and Buck cover the two running backs. The strong safety covers the tight end, and the free safety is free.

STRONG SAFETY: Lines up inside shade on the tight end, four to five yards deep. Covers the tight end.

STUD: Lines up in an 8 technique. Rushes hard from the outside. Contains the quarterback and strongside run. Chases weakside run.

STRONG END: Slants across the offensive tackle's face into the B gap.

MIKE: Has no strongside gap responsibilities. Checks both A gaps as he pursues the ball from an inside-out position versus weakside run. Covers the near back versus pass.

NOSE: Loops across the offensive tackle's face into the strongside C gap.

BUCK: Scrapes outside and contains the play versus weakside run. Checks both A gaps as he pursues the ball from an inside-out position versus strongside run. Covers the near back versus pass.

WEAK END: Slants across the offensive tackle's face into the B gap.

WHIP: Rushes through the outside shoulder of the offensive tackle. Secures the C gap and contains the quarterback.

FREE SAFETY: Free. Plays centerfield. Provides alley support versus run.

STRONG CORNER: Covers receiver #1. Inside/outside technique is dependent upon field position and the distance of the flanker's split.

WEAK CORNER: Covers receiver #1. Inside/outside technique is dependent upon field position and the distance of the split end's split.

STUNT #29

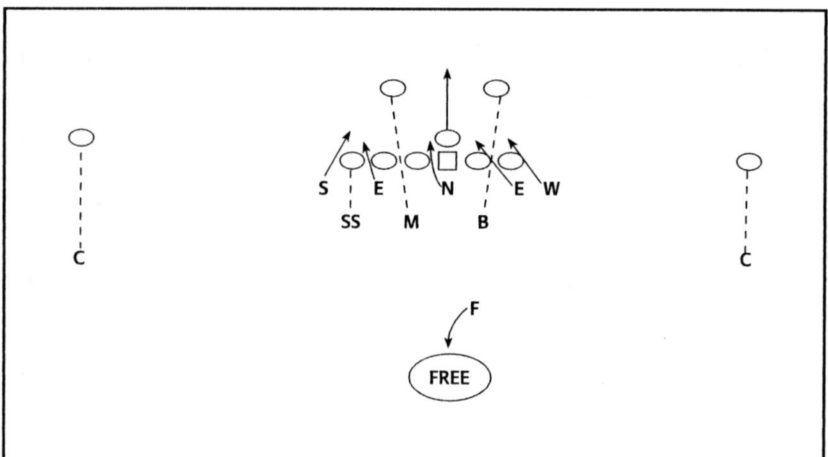

STUNT DESCRIPTION: This is a simple dog that features a strongside line slant.

SECONDARY COVERAGE: Cover 1. Mike and Buck cover the two running backs. The strong safety covers the tight end, and the free safety is free.

STRONG SAFETY: Lines up inside shade on the tight end, four to five yards deep. Covers the tight end.

STUD: Lines up in an 8 technique. Rushes hard from the outside. Contains the quarterback and strongside run. Chases weakside run.

STRONG END: Slants to the C gap.

MIKE: Fills the B gap versus strongside run. Checks the weakside A gap as he pursues weakside run from an inside-out position. Covers the near back versus pass.

NOSE: Slants to the strongside A gap.

BUCK: Scrapes outside and contains the play versus weakside run. Checks the weakside A gap as he pursues the ball from an inside-out position versus strongside run. Covers the near back versus pass.

WEAK END: Slants across the offensive tackle's face into the B gap.

WHIP: Rushes through the outside shoulder of the offensive tackle. Secures the C gap and contains the quarterback.

FREE SAFETY: Free. Plays centerfield. Provides alley support versus run.

STRONG CORNER: Covers receiver #1. Inside/outside technique is dependent upon field position and the distance of the flanker's split.

WEAK CORNER: Covers receiver #1. Inside/outside technique is dependent upon field position and the distance of the split end's split.

STUNT #30

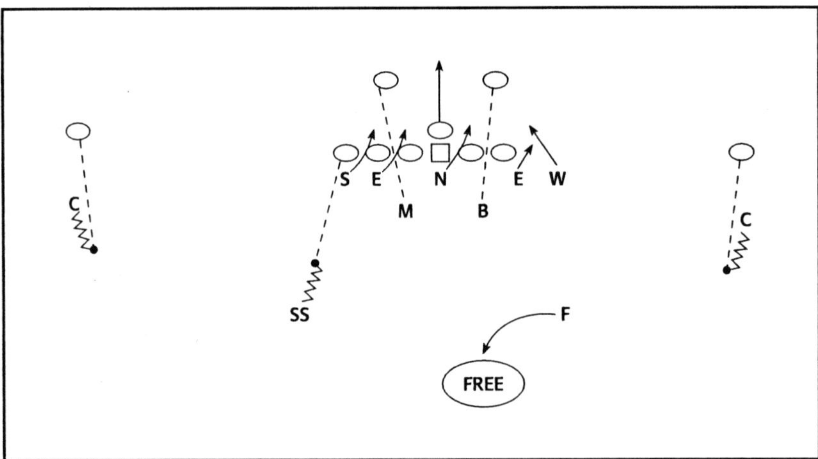

STUNT DESCRIPTION: This is a simple dog that features a weakside line slant.

SECONDARY COVERAGE: Cover 1 disguised as cover 2. Mike and Buck cover the two running backs. The strong safety covers the tight end, and the free safety is free.

STRONG SAFETY: Lines up as though he's playing cover 2. During cadence, he moves to a position that enables him to cover the tight end. If the tight end blocks, the strong safety comes up quickly and contains.

STUD: Slants across the tight end's face into the C gap. Secures the C gap and contains the quarterback.

STRONG END: Slants into the B gap.

MIKE: Has no strongside gap responsibility. Pursues strongside run from an inside-out position. Checks the strongside A gap as he shuffles down the line versus weakside run. Covers the near back versus pass.

NOSE: Slants to the weakside A gap.

BUCK: Plugs the B gap versus weakside run. Checks the strongside A gap as he pursues the ball from an inside-out position versus strongside run. Covers the near back versus pass.

WEAK END: Slants into the C gap.

WHIP: Rushes from the edge. Contains the quarterback and weakside run. Chases strongside run.

FREE SAFETY: Free. Plays centerfield. Disguises his assignment from a cover 2 look. Provides alley support versus run.

STRONG CORNER: Covers receiver #1. Inside/outside technique is dependent upon field position and the distance of the flanker's split.

WEAK CORNER: Covers receiver #1. Inside/outside technique is dependent upon field position and the distance of the split end's split.

STUNT #31

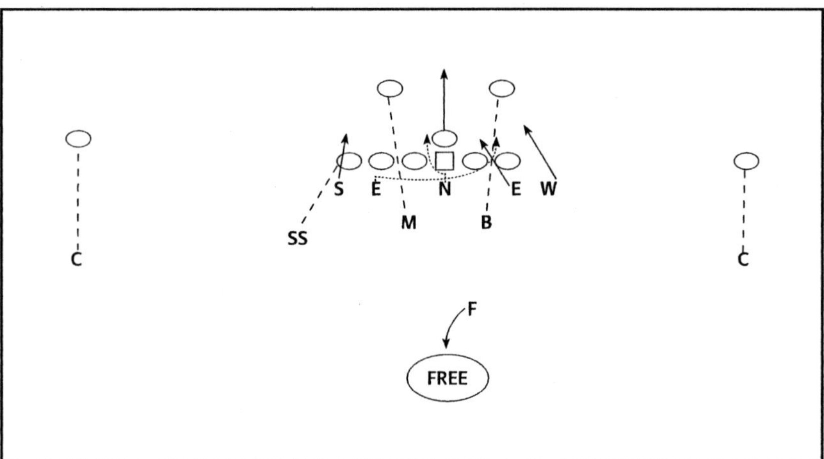

STUNT DESCRIPTION: This is a simple dog that incorporates a delayed line twist.

SECONDARY COVERAGE: Cover 1 disguised as cover 3. Mike and Buck cover the two running backs. The strong safety covers the tight end, and the free safety is free.

STRONG SAFETY: Lines up as though he's playing cover 3 sky. If the tight end releases, the strong safety covers him. If he blocks, the strong safety comes up quickly and contains.

STUD: Plays 9 technique and contains the quarterback.

STRONG END: Plays 5 technique versus run. Loops across the face of the offensive guard into the weakside B gap versus pass.

MIKE: Plays base technique versus run. Covers the near back versus pass.

NOSE: Plays 0 technique versus run. Quickly penetrates the strongside A gap versus pass.

BUCK: Plays base technique versus run. Covers the near back versus pass.

WEAK END: Slants across the face of the offensive tackle into the B gap.

WHIP: Rushes from the outside. Contains the quarterback and weakside run. Chases strongside run.

FREE SAFETY: Free. Plays centerfield. Provides alley support versus run.

STRONG CORNER: Covers receiver #1. Inside/outside technique is dependent upon field position and the distance of the flanker's split.

WEAK CORNER: Covers receiver #1. Inside/outside technique is dependent upon field position and the distance of the split end's split.

STUNT #32

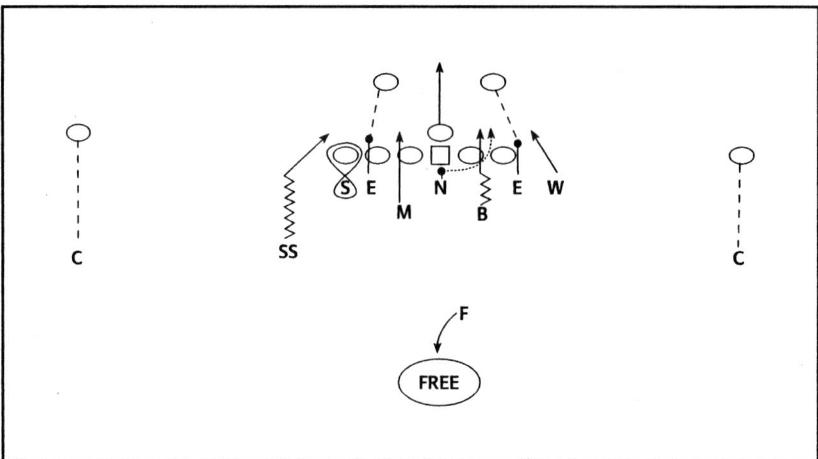

STUNT DESCRIPTION: This seven-man illusion stunt incorporates a strong safety blitz and a delayed twin rush by the nose.

SECONDARY COVERAGE: Cover 1, disguised as cover 3. Both ends spy the near backs. The strong safety blitzes, Stud covers the tight end, and the free safety is free.

STRONG SAFETY: Creeps toward the line during cadence. Rushes from the outside. Contains the quarterback and strongside run, and chases weakside run.

STUD: Covers the tight end (inside funnel).

STRONG END: Plays 5 technique versus run. Spies the near back versus pass.

MIKE: Blitzes through the outside shoulder of the guard and secures the B gap.

NOSE: Plays 0 technique versus run. Delay rushes (twin) through the weakside B gap versus pass.

BUCK: Creeps toward the line during cadence and blitzes through the outside shoulder of the guard.

WEAK END: Plays 5 technique versus run. Spies the near back versus pass.

WHIP: Rushes outside. Contains the quarterback and weakside run. Chases strongside run.

FREE SAFETY: Free. Plays centerfield. Provides alley support versus run.

STRONG CORNER: Covers receiver #1. Inside/outside technique is dependent upon field position and the distance of the flanker's split.

WEAK CORNER: Covers receiver #1. Inside/outside technique is dependent upon field position and the distance of the split end's split.

STUNT #33

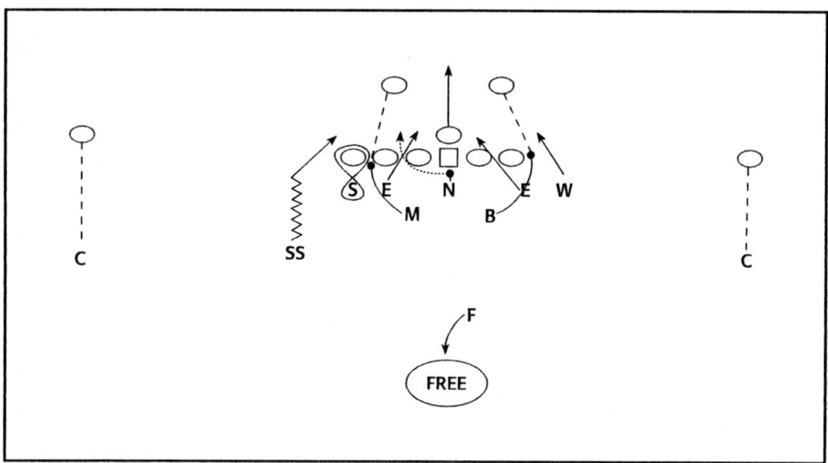

STUNT DESCRIPTION: This stunt gives the **illusion** of a seven-man pass rush. It incorporates a strong safety blitz and a delayed twin rush by the nose.

SECONDARY COVERAGE: Cover 1 disguised as cover 3. Mike and Buck cover the two running backs. Stud covers the tight end, the strong safety blitzes, and the free safety is free.

STRONG SAFETY: Creeps toward the line during cadence. Rushes from the outside and contains the quarterback and strongside run. Chases weakside run.

STUD: Covers the tight end (inside funnel).

STRONG END: Slants across the tackle's face into the B gap.

MIKE: Fakes a blitz toward the C gap. Secures the C gap and spies the near back.

NOSE: Plays 0 technique versus run. Delay rushes (twin) through the strongside B gap versus pass.

BUCK: Fakes a blitz toward the C gap. Secures the C gap and spies the near back.

WEAK END: Slants across the offensive tackle's face into the B gap.

WHIP: Rushes from the edge. Contains the quarterback and weakside run. Chases strongside run.

FREE SAFETY: Free. Plays centerfield. Provides alley support versus run.

STRONG CORNER: Covers receiver #1. Inside/outside technique is dependent upon field position and the distance of the flanker's split.

WEAK CORNER: Covers receiver #1. Inside/outside technique is dependent upon field position and the distance of the split end's split.

STUNT #34

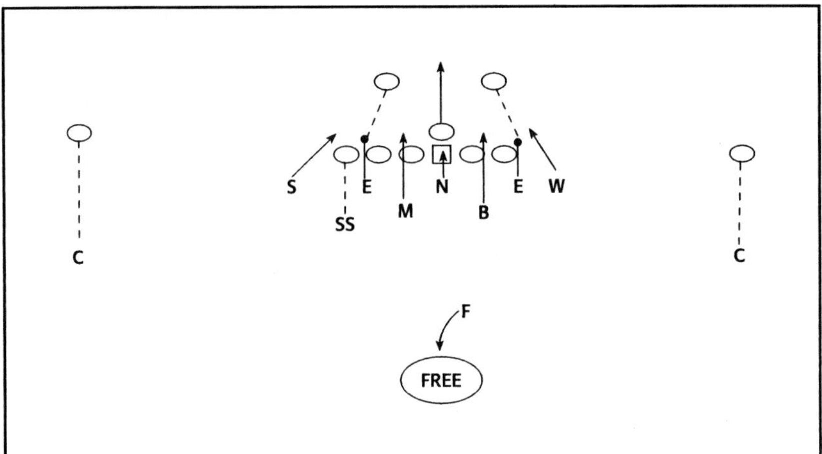

STUNT DESCRIPTION: This is an illusion stunt that gives the **illusion** of a seven-man pass rush.

SECONDARY COVERAGE: Cover 1. Both ends spy the near running back. The strong safety covers the tight end, and the free safety is free. Possible variation: Stud and Whip spy the near backs.

STRONG SAFETY: Lines up inside shade on the tight end, four to five yards deep. Covers the tight end.

STUD: Lines up in an 8 technique. Rushes hard from the outside. Contains the quarterback and strongside run. Chases weakside run.

STRONG END: Plays 5 technique versus run. Spies the near back versus pass.

MIKE: Blitzes through the outside shoulder of the guard and secures the B gap.

NOSE: Plays 0 technique.

BUCK: Blitzes through the outside shoulder of the offensive guard and secures the C gap.

WEAK END: Plays 5 technique versus run. Spies the near back versus pass.

WHIP: Rushes hard from the outside. Contains the quarterback and weakside run. Chases strongside run.

FREE SAFETY: Free. Plays centerfield. Provides alley support versus run.

STRONG CORNER: Covers receiver #1. Inside/outside technique is dependent upon field position and the distance of the flanker's split.

WEAK CORNER: Covers receiver #1. Inside/outside technique is dependent upon field position and the distance of the split end's split.

STUNT #35

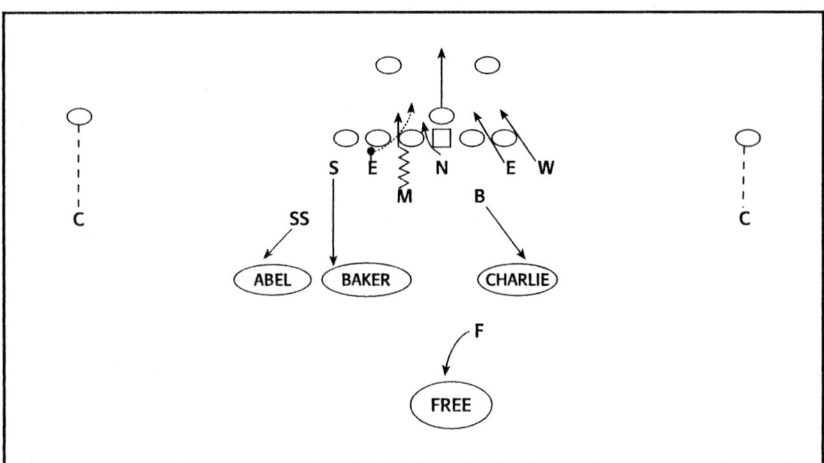

STUNT DESCRIPTION: This banjo stunt features a delayed twin rush by the strongside end.

SECONDARY COVERAGE: Cover 1 disguised as cover 3. The strong safety, Stud, and Buck drop off into banjo coverage.

STRONG SAFETY: Lines up as though he's playing cover 3 sky. Keys the tight end. If he blocks, the strong safety quickly supports strongside run. Drops **Abel** banjo versus dropback pass. Checks the tight end for throwback before pursuing weakside run.

STUD: Plays 9 technique versus run. Drops **Baker** banjo versus pass.

STRONG END: Plays 5 technique versus run. Delay rushes (twin) through the strongside B gap versus pass.

MIKE: Creeps toward the line during cadence. Blitzes hard through the outside shoulder of the guard as the ball is being snapped and secures the B gap.

NOSE: Slants into the strongside A gap.

BUCK: Scrapes outside and contains versus weakside run. Pursues the ball from an inside-out position versus strongside run. Drops **Charlie** banjo versus pass.

WEAK END: Slants across the offensive tackle's face into the B gap.

WHIP: Rushes through the outside shoulder of the offensive tackle. Secures the C gap and contains the quarterback.

FREE SAFETY: Free. Plays centerfield. Provides alley support versus run.

STRONG CORNER: Covers receiver #1. Inside/outside technique is dependent upon field position and the distance of the flanker's split.

WEAK CORNER: Covers receiver #1. Inside/outside technique is dependent upon field position and the distance of the split end's split.

STUNT #36

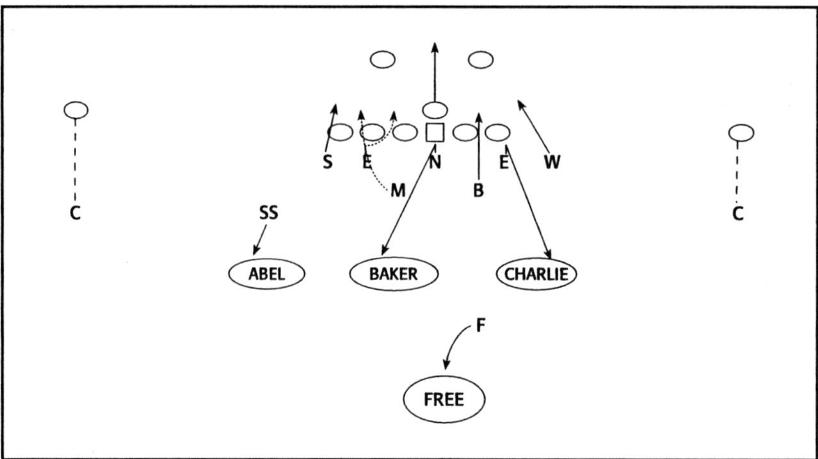

STUNT DESCRIPTION: This banjo stunt features a delayed blitz by Mike.

SECONDARY COVERAGE: Cover 1 disguised as cover 3. The strong safety, nose, and the weak end drop off into banjo coverage, and the free safety is free.

STRONG SAFETY: Lines up as though he's playing cover 3. Keys the tight end. If he blocks, the strong safety quickly supports strongside run. Drops **Abel** banjo versus dropback pass. Checks the tight end for throwback before pursuing weakside run.

STUD: Plays 9 technique versus run. Contains rush versus pass.

STRONG END: Plays 5 technique versus run. Slants across the face of the offensive tackle into the B gap versus pass.

MIKE: Plays base technique versus run. Delay-blitzes through the outside shoulder of the offensive tackle versus pass.

NOSE: Plays 0 technique versus run. Drops **Baker** banjo versus pass.

BUCK: Blitzes through the outside shoulder of the offensive guard and secures the B gap.

WEAK END: Plays 5 technique versus run. Drops **Charlie** banjo versus pass.

WHIP: Rushes hard from the outside. Contains the quarterback and weakside run. Chases strongside run.

FREE SAFETY: Free. Plays centerfield. Provides alley support versus run.

STRONG CORNER: Covers receiver #1. Inside/outside technique is dependent upon field position and the distance of the flanker's split.

WEAK CORNER: Covers receiver #1. Inside/outside technique is dependent upon field position and the distance of the split end's split.

STUNT #37

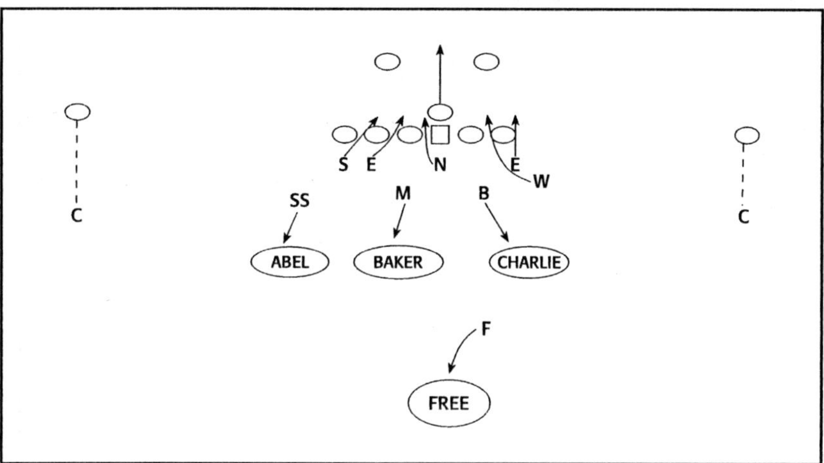

STUNT DESCRIPTION: This is a banjo blitz that has both outside linebackers rushing.

SECONDARY COVERAGE: Cover 1 disguised as cover 3. Mike, Buck, and the strong safety drop off into banjo coverage, and the free safety plays centerfield.

STRONG SAFETY: Lines up as though he's playing cover 3. Keys the tight end. If he blocks, the strong safety quickly supports strongside run. Drops **Abel** banjo versus dropback pass. Checks the tight end for throwback before pursuing weakside run.

STUD: Slants across the tight end's face into the C gap. Secures the C gap and contains the quarterback.

STRONG END: Slants into the B gap.

MIKE: Has no strongside gap responsibility. Pursues strongside run from an inside-out position. Checks the weakside A gap as he shuffles down the line versus weakside run. Drops **Baker** banjo versus pass.

NOSE: Slants to the strongside A gap.

BUCK: Scrapes outside and contains versus weakside run. Checks the weakside A gap as he pursues the ball from an inside-out position versus strongside run. Drops **Charlie** banjo versus pass.

WEAK END: Plays 5 technique versus run. Contains the quarterback versus pass.

WHIP: Blitzes through the B gap.

FREE SAFETY: Free. Plays centerfield. Provides alley support versus run.

STRONG CORNER: Covers receiver #1. Inside/outside technique is dependent upon field position and the distance of the flanker's split.

WEAK CORNER: Covers receiver #1. Inside/outside technique is dependent upon field position and the distance of the split end's split.

STUNT #38

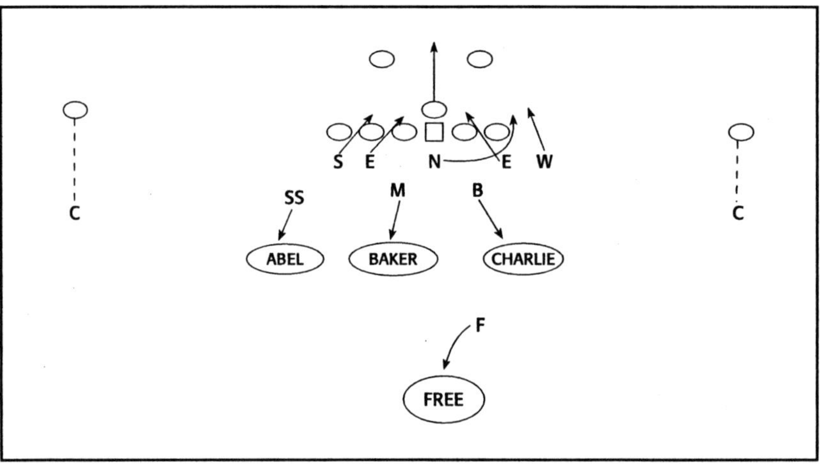

STUNT DESCRIPTION: This is a banjo blitz that has both outside linebackers rushing.

SECONDARY COVERAGE: Cover 1 disguised as cover 3. Mike, Buck, and the strong safety drop off into banjo coverage, and the free safety plays centerfield.

STRONG SAFETY: Lines up as though he's playing cover 3. Keys the tight end. If he blocks, the strong safety quickly supports strongside run. Drops **Abel** banjo versus dropback pass. Checks the tight end for throwback before pursuing weakside run.

STUD: Slants across the tight end's face into the C gap. Secures the C gap and contains the quarterback.

STRONG END: Slants into the B gap.

MIKE: Has no strongside gap responsibility. Pursues strongside run from an inside-out position. Checks both A gaps as he shuffles down the line versus weakside run. Drops **Baker** banjo versus pass.

NOSE: Loops across the face of the offensive tackle and secures the weakside C gap.

BUCK: Pursues the ball from an inside-out position versus weakside run. Checks both A gaps as he shuffles down the line versus strongside run. Drops **Charlie** banjo versus pass.

WEAK END: Slants into the B gap.

WHIP: Rushes from the edge. Contains the quarterback and weakside run. Chases strongside run.

FREE SAFETY: Free. Plays centerfield. Provides alley support versus run.

STRONG CORNER: Covers receiver #1. Inside/outside technique is dependent upon field position and the distance of the flanker's split.

WEAK CORNER: Covers receiver #1. Inside/outside technique is dependent upon field position and the distance of the split end's split.

STUNT #39

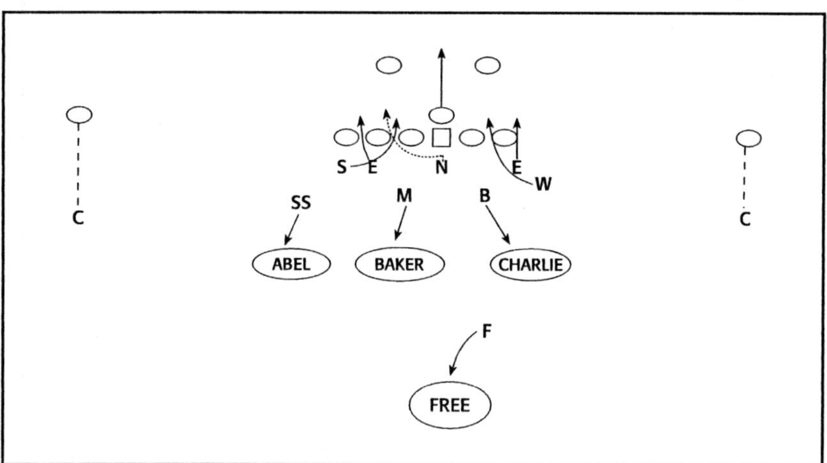

STUNT DESCRIPTION: This is a banjo blitz that has both outside linebackers rushing; it is enhanced by a delayed line twist (twin stunt) by the nose.

SECONDARY COVERAGE: Cover 1 disguised as cover 3. Mike, Buck, and the strong safety drop off into banjo coverage, and the free safety plays centerfield.

STRONG SAFETY: Lines up as though he's playing cover 3. Keys the tight end. If he blocks, the strong safety quickly supports strongside run. Drops **Abel** banjo versus dropback pass. Checks the tight end for throwback before pursuing weakside run.

STUD: Loops through the B gap.

STRONG END: Penetrates into the C gap at the snap. Secures the C gap and contains the quarterback.

MIKE: Has no strongside gap responsibility. Pursues strongside run from an inside-out position. Versus weakside run, checks the strongside A gap as he shuffles down the line. Drops **Baker** banjo versus pass.

NOSE: Plays 0 technique versus run. Versus pass, slants across the face of the offensive guard into the strongside B gap (twin stunt).

BUCK: Scrapes outside and contains versus weakside run. Pursues the ball from an inside-out position versus strongside run. Drops **Charlie** banjo versus pass.

WEAK END: Plays 5 technique versus run. Contains quarterback versus pass.

WHIP: Blitzes through the B gap.

FREE SAFETY: Free. Plays centerfield. Provides alley support versus run.

STRONG CORNER: Covers receiver #1. Inside/outside technique is dependent upon field position and the distance of the flanker's split.

WEAK CORNER: Covers receiver #1. Inside/outside technique is dependent upon field position and the distance of the split end's split.

STUNT #40

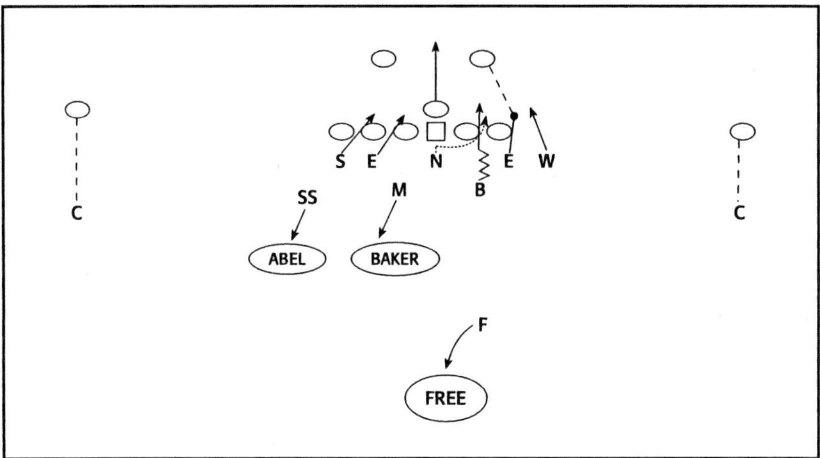

STUNT DESCRIPTION: This is a gumbo blitz that has both outside linebackers rushing and a delayed twin rush by the nose.

SECONDARY COVERAGE: Cover 1 disguised as cover 3. Mike and the strong safety drop off into gumbo coverage, the weak end spies the near back, and the free safety plays centerfield.

STRONG SAFETY: Lines up as though he's playing cover 3. Keys the tight end. If he blocks, the strong safety quickly supports strongside run. Drops **Abel** banjo versus dropback pass. Checks the tight end for throwback before pursuing weakside run.

STUD: Slants across the face of the tight end. Secures the C gap and contains the quarterback.

STRONG END: Slants into the B gap.

MIKE: Has no gap responsibility. Pursues strongside and weakside run from an inside-out position. Drops **Baker** banjo versus pass.

NOSE: Plays 0 technique versus run. Slants across the offensive guard's face into the weakside B gap (twin stunt) versus pass.

BUCK: Creeps toward the line during cadence and blitzes through the outside shoulder of the offensive guard at the snap.

WEAK END: Plays 5 technique versus run. Spies the near back versus pass.

WHIP: Rushes from the edge. Contains the quarterback and weakside run. Chases strongside run.

FREE SAFETY: Free. Plays centerfield. Provides alley support versus run.

STRONG CORNER: Covers receiver #1. Inside/outside technique is dependent upon field position and the distance of the flanker's split.

WEAK CORNER: Covers receiver #1. Inside/outside technique is dependent upon field position and the distance of the split end's split.

STUNT #41

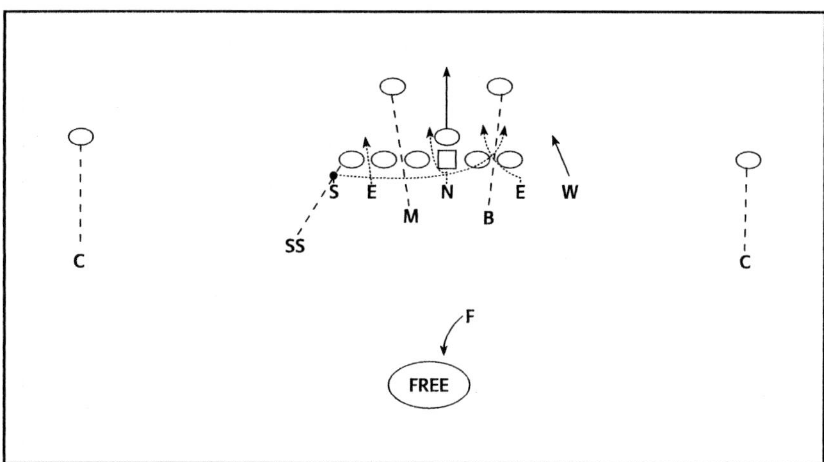

STUNT DESCRIPTION: This dog features delayed line twists versus pass.

SECONDARY COVERAGE: Cover 1 disguised as cover 3. Mike and Buck cover the near backs, the strong safety covers the tight end, and the free safety plays centerfield.

STRONG SAFETY: Lines up as though he's playing cover 3 sky and covers the tight end.

STUD: Plays 9 technique versus run. Loops into the weakside B gap (twin stunt) versus pass.

STRONG END: Penetrates the C gap at the snap. Secures the C gap and contains the quarterback.

MIKE: Plays base technique versus run. Covers the near back versus pass.

NOSE: Plays 0 technique versus run. Quickly penetrates the strongside A gap versus pass.

BUCK: Plays base technique versus run. Covers the near back versus pass

WEAK END: Plays 5 technique versus run. Slants across the tackle's face and penetrates the B gap versus pass.

WHIP: Rushes from the edge. Contains the quarterback and weakside run. Chases strongside run.

FREE SAFETY: Free. Plays centerfield. Provides alley support versus run.

STRONG CORNER: Covers receiver #1. Inside/outside technique is dependent upon field position and the distance of the flanker's split.

WEAK CORNER: Covers receiver #1. Inside/outside technique is dependent upon field position and the distance of the split end's split.

STUNT #42

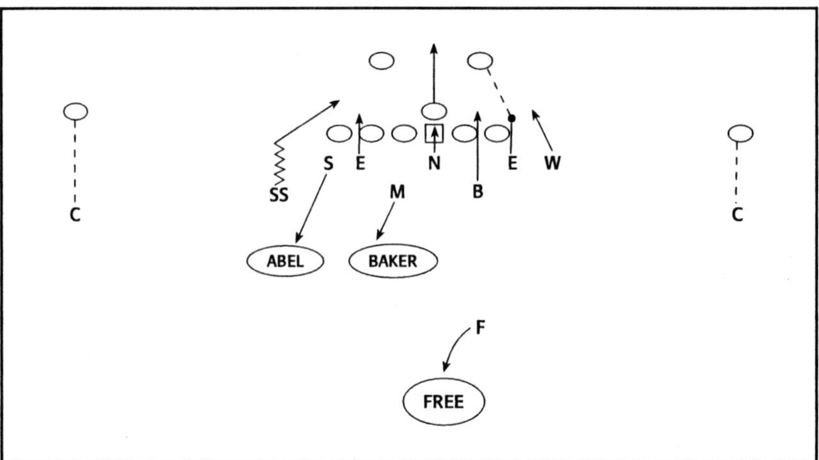

STUNT DESCRIPTION: This gumbo blitz has the strong safety rushing from the edge.

SECONDARY COVERAGE: Cover 1 disguised as cover 3. Mike and Stud drop off into gumbo coverage, the weak end spies the near back, and the free safety plays centerfield.

STRONG SAFETY: Lines up as though he's playing cover 3 sky. Creeps toward the line during cadence and rushes hard from the edge. Contains the quarterback and strongside run. Chases weakside run.

STUD: Plays 9 technique versus run. Drops **Abel** gumbo versus pass.

STRONG END: Plays 5 technique.

MIKE: Plays base technique versus run. Drops **Baker** gumbo versus pass.

NOSE: Plays 0 technique.

BUCK: Blitzes through the outside shoulder of the offensive guard and secures the B gap.

WEAK END: Plays 5 technique versus run. Spies the near back versus pass.

WHIP: Rushes from the edge. Contains the quarterback and weakside run. Chases strongside run.

FREE SAFETY: Free. Plays centerfield. Provides alley support versus run.

STRONG CORNER: Covers receiver #1. Inside/outside technique is dependent upon field position and the distance of the flanker's split.

WEAK CORNER: Covers receiver #1. Inside/outside technique is dependent upon field position and the distance of the split end's split.

STUNT #43

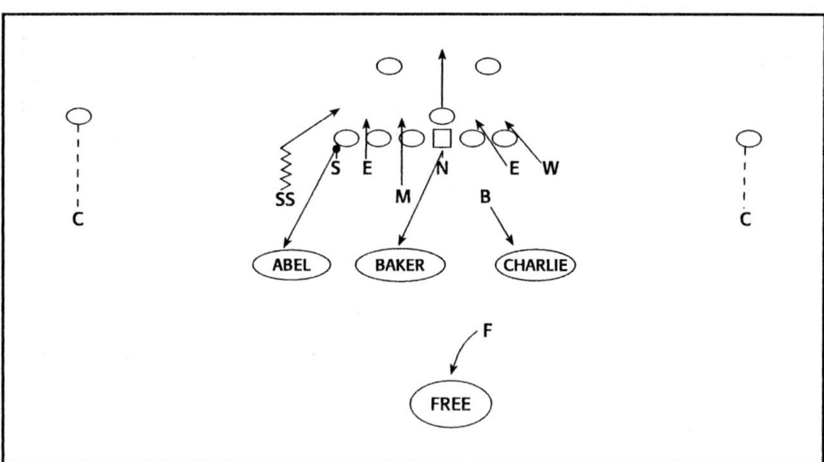

STUNT DESCRIPTION: This banjo blitz has the strong safety rushing from the edge.

SECONDARY COVERAGE: Cover 1 disguised as cover 3. Stud, nose, and Buck drop off into banjo coverage, and the free safety plays centerfield.

STRONG SAFETY: Lines up as though he's playing cover 3 sky. Creeps toward the line during cadence and rushes hard from the edge. Contains the quarterback and strongside run. Chases weakside run.

STUD: Plays 9 technique versus run. Drops **Abel** banjo versus pass.

STRONG END: Plays 5 technique.

MIKE: Blitzes through the outside shoulder of the offensive guard and secures the B gap.

NOSE: Plays 0 technique versus run. Drops **Baker** banjo versus pass.

BUCK: Has no strongside gap responsibility. Scrapes outside and contains versus weakside run. Drops **Charlie** banjo versus pass.

WEAK END: Slants across the offensive tackle's face into the B gap.

WHIP: Rushes through the outside shoulder of the offensive tackle. Secures the C gap and contains the quarterback.

FREE SAFETY: Free. Plays centerfield. Provides alley support versus run.

STRONG CORNER: Covers receiver #1. Inside/outside technique is dependent upon field position and the distance of the flanker's split.

WEAK CORNER: Covers receiver #1. Inside/outside technique is dependent upon field position and the distance of the split end's split.

STUNT #44

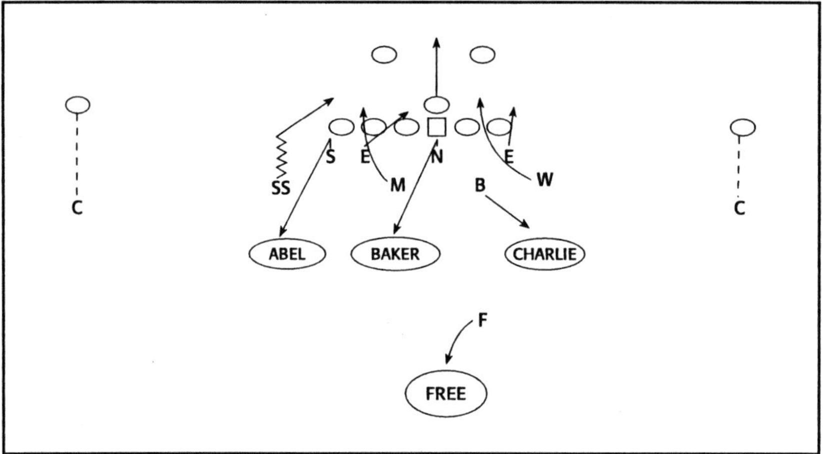

STUNT DESCRIPTION: This banjo blitz has the strong safety rushing from the edge.

SECONDARY COVERAGE: Cover 1 disguised as cover 3. Stud, nose, and Buck drop off into banjo coverage, and the free safety plays centerfield.

STRONG SAFETY: Lines up as though he's playing cover 3 sky. Creeps toward the line during cadence and rushes hard from the edge. Contains the quarterback and strongside run. Chases weakside run.

STUD: Plays 9 technique versus run. Drops **Abel** banjo versus pass.

STRONG END: Slants across the offensive tackle's face into the B gap.

MIKE: Blitzes through the outside shoulder of the offensive tackle and secures the C gap.

NOSE: Plays 0 technique versus run. Drops **Baker** banjo versus pass.

BUCK: Scrapes outside and contains versus weakside run. Pursues strongside run from an inside-out position. Drops **Charlie** banjo versus pass.

WEAK END: Plays 5 technique versus run. Contains the quarterback versus pass.

WHIP: Blitzes through the B gap.

FREE SAFETY: Free. Plays centerfield. Provides alley support versus run.

STRONG CORNER: Covers receiver #1. Inside/outside technique is dependent upon field position and the distance of the flanker's split.

WEAK CORNER: Covers receiver #1. Inside/outside technique is dependent upon field position and the distance of the split end's split.

STUNT #45

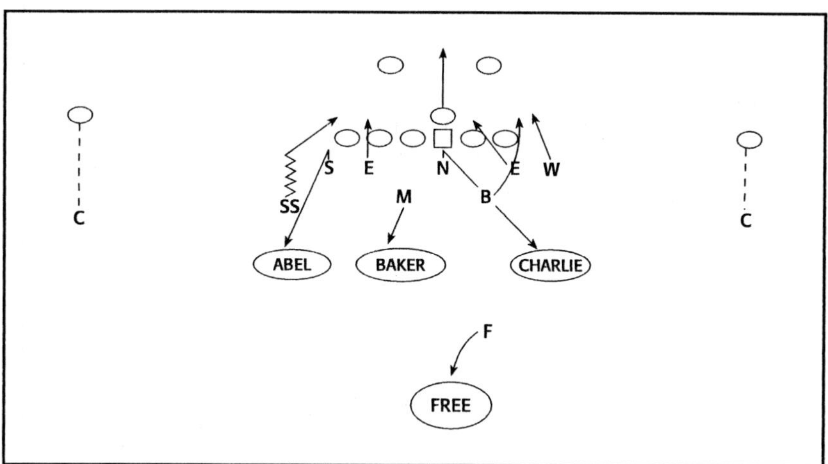

STUNT DESCRIPTION: This banjo blitz has the strong safety rushing from the edge.

SECONDARY COVERAGE: Cover 1 disguised as cover 3. Stud, Mike, and nose drop off into banjo coverage, and the free safety plays centerfield.

STRONG SAFETY: Lines up as though he's playing cover 3 sky. Creeps toward the line during cadence and rushes hard from the edge. Contains the quarterback and strongside run. Chases weakside run.

STUD: Plays 9 technique versus run. Drops **Abel** banjo versus pass.

STRONG END: Plays 5 technique.

MIKE: Plays base technique versus run. Drops **Baker** banjo versus pass.

NOSE: Plays 0 technique versus run. Drops **Charlie** banjo versus pass.

BUCK: Blitzes through the outside shoulder of the offensive tackle and secures the C gap.

WEAK END: Slants across the offensive tackle's face into the B gap.

WHIP: Rushes hard from the edge. Contains the quarterback and weakside run. Chases strongside run.

FREE SAFETY: Free. Plays centerfield. Provides alley support versus run.

STRONG CORNER: Covers receiver #1. Inside/outside technique is dependent upon field position and the distance of the flanker's split.

WEAK CORNER: Covers receiver #1. Inside/outside technique is dependent upon field position and the distance of the split end's split.

STUNT #46

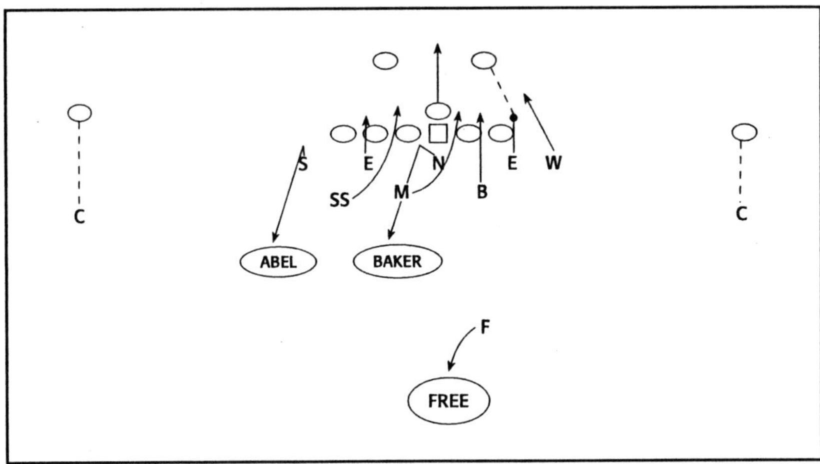

STUNT DESCRIPTION: This gumbo blitz gives the **illusion** of an eight-man pass rush.

SECONDARY COVERAGE: Cover 1. Stud and nose drop off into gumbo coverage, and the weak end spies the near back. The free safety plays centerfield.

STRONG SAFETY: Lines up inside shade on the tight end, 4 to 5 yards deep. Blitzes through the B gap at the snap.

STUD: Plays 8 technique versus run. Drops **Abel** gumbo versus pass.

STRONG END: Plays 5 technique versus run. Contains the quarterback versus pass.

MIKE: Blitzes through the weakside A gap.

NOSE: Slants into the strongside A gap. Secures the A gap versus run and drops **Baker** gumbo versus pass.

BUCK: Blitzes through the outside shoulder of the offensive guard and secures the B gap.

WEAK END: Plays 5 technique versus run. Spies the near back versus pass.

WHIP: Rushes from the edge. Contains the quarterback and strongside run. Chases weakside run.

FREE SAFETY: Free. Plays centerfield. Provides alley support versus run.

STRONG CORNER: Covers receiver #1. Inside/outside technique is dependent upon field position and the distance of the flanker's split.

WEAK CORNER: Covers receiver #1. Inside/outside technique is dependent upon field position and the distance of the split end's split.

STUNT #47

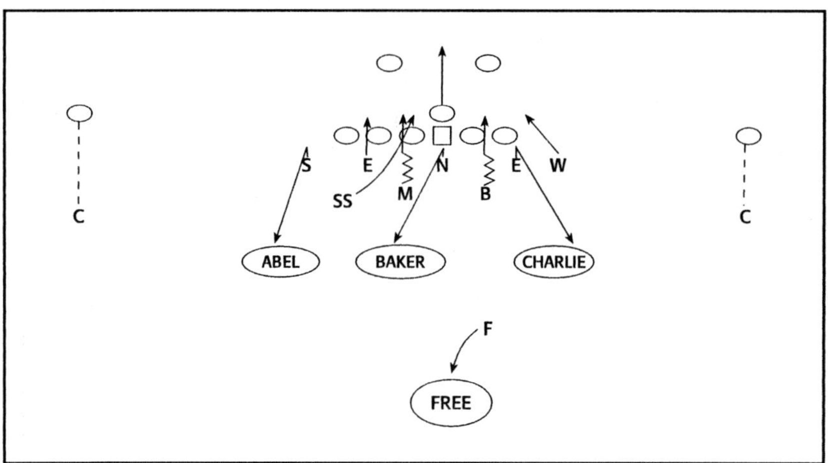

STUNT DESCRIPTION: This banjo blitz features a strong safety blitz and a twin stunt through the strongside B gap.

SECONDARY COVERAGE: Cover 1. Stud, nose, and the weak end drop off into banjo coverage, and the free safety is free.

STRONG SAFETY: Lines up inside shade on the tight end, 4 to 5 yards deep. Blitzes through the B gap at the snap.

STUD: Plays 8 technique versus run. Drops **Abel** banjo versus pass.

STRONG END: Plays 5 technique versus run. Contains the quarterback versus pass.

MIKE: Creeps toward the line during cadence and blitzes through the outside shoulder of the guard at the snap.

NOSE: Plays 0 technique versus run. Drops **Baker** banjo versus pass.

BUCK: Creeps toward the line during cadence and blitzes through the outside shoulder of the offensive guard. Secures the B gap.

WEAK END: Plays 5 technique versus run. Drops **Charlie** banjo versus pass.

WHIP: Rushes from the edge. Contains the quarterback and weakside run. Chases strongside run.

FREE SAFETY: Free. Plays centerfield. Provides alley support versus run.

STRONG CORNER: Covers receiver #1. Inside/outside technique is dependent upon field position and the distance of the flanker's split.

WEAK CORNER: Covers receiver #1. Inside/outside technique is dependent upon field position and the distance of the split end's split.

STUNT #48

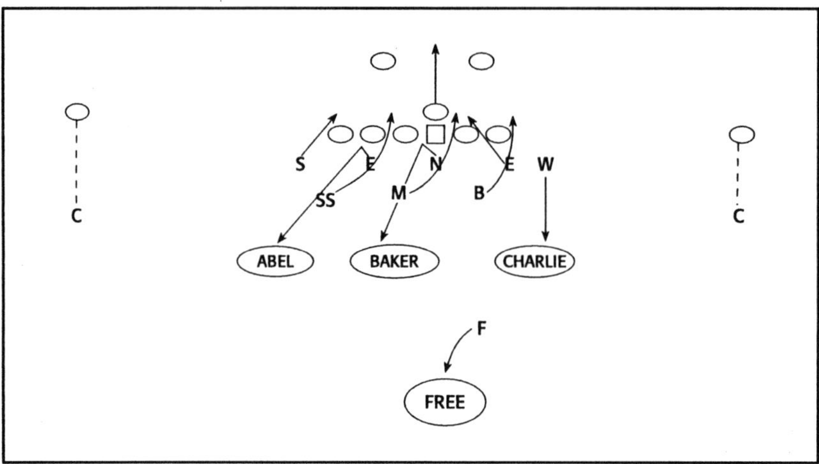

STUNT DESCRIPTION: This banjo blitz gives the **illusion** of a seven-man pass rush.

SECONDARY COVERAGE: Cover 1. The strong end, nose, and Whip drop off into banjo coverage, and the free safety is free.

STRONG SAFETY: Lines up inside shade on the tight end, 4 to 5 yards deep. Blitzes through the B gap.

STUD: Lines up in an 8 technique. Rushes hard from the outside. Contains the quarterback and strongside run. Chases weakside run.

STRONG END: Plays 5 technique versus run. Drops **Abel** banjo versus pass.

MIKE: Blitzes through the weakside A gap.

NOSE: Slants to and secures the strongside A gap versus run. Drops **Baker** banjo versus pass.

BUCK: Blitzes through the outside shoulder of the offensive tackle. Secures the C gap and contains the quarterback.

WEAK END: Slants across the face of the offensive tackle into the B gap.

WHIP: Plays 9 technique versus run. Drops **Charlie** banjo versus pass.

FREE SAFETY: Free. Plays centerfield. Provides alley support versus run.

STRONG CORNER: Covers receiver #1. Inside/outside technique is dependent upon field position and the distance of the flanker's split.

WEAK CORNER: Covers receiver #1. Inside/outside technique is dependent upon field position and the distance of the split end's split.

STUNT #49

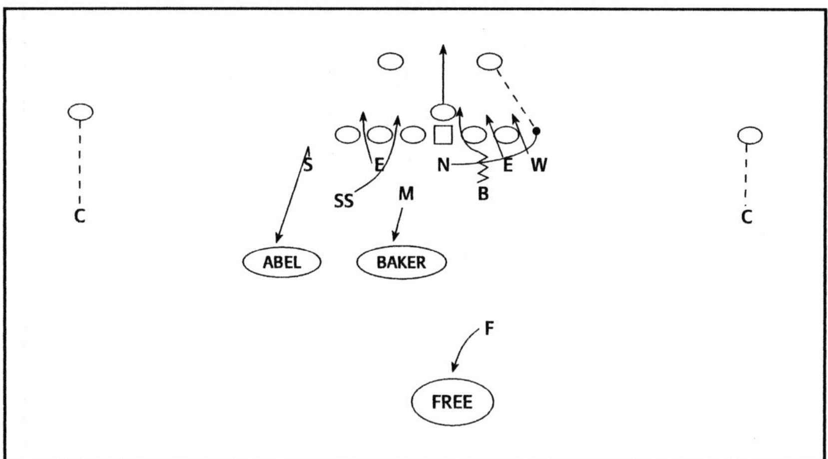

STUNT DESCRIPTION: This gumbo blitz has the strong safety blitzing through the B gap.

SECONDARY COVERAGE: Cover 1. Stud and Mike drop off into gumbo coverage, the nose spies the near back, and the free safety is free.

STRONG SAFETY: Lines up inside shade on the tight end, 4 to 5 yards deep. Blitzes through the B gap.

STUD: Plays 8 technique versus run. Drops **Abel** gumbo versus pass.

STRONG END: Slants to the C gap and contains the quarterback.

MIKE: Plays base technique versus run. Drops **Baker** gumbo versus pass.

NOSE: Loops across the face of the offensive tackle. Contains weakside run and spies the near back.

BUCK: Creeps toward the line during cadence. Convinces the offensive guard that he's going to blitz through the guard's outside shoulder, but blitzes through the weakside A gap as the ball is snapped.

WEAK END: Slants across the face of the offensive tackle into the B gap.

WHIP: Rushes through the outside shoulder of the offensive tackle. Secures the C gap and contains the quarterback.

FREE SAFETY: Free. Plays centerfield. Provides alley support versus run.

STRONG CORNER: Covers receiver #1. Inside/outside technique is dependent upon field position and the distance of the flanker's split.

WEAK CORNER: Covers receiver #1. Inside/outside technique is dependent upon field position and the distance of the split end's split.

STUNT #50

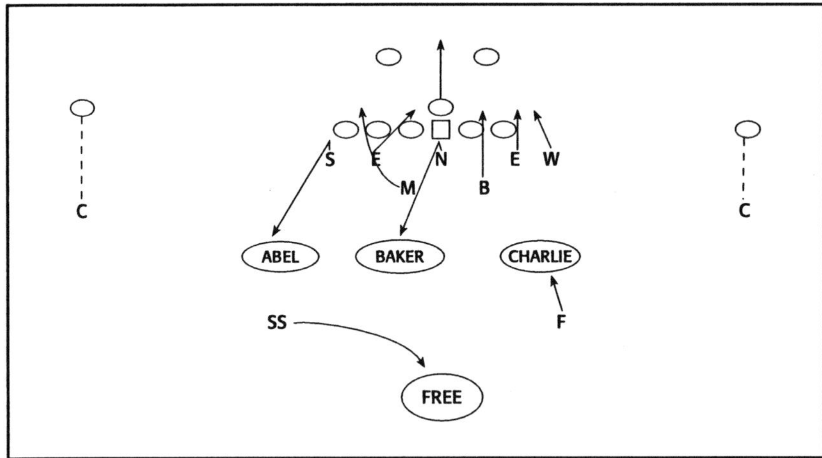

STUNT DESCRIPTION: This banjo blitz gives the **illusion** of a six-man pass rush.

SECONDARY COVERAGE: Cover 1 disguised as cover 2. Stud, nose and the free safety drop off into banjo coverage, and the strong safety is free.

STRONG SAFETY: Lines up as though he's playing cover 2. Drops to centerfield versus pass. Comes up quickly and contains versus strongside run. Checks throwback first, and then pursues versus weakside run.

STUD: Plays 9 technique versus run. Drops **Abel** banjo versus pass.

STRONG END: Slants into the B gap.

MIKE: Blitzes through the outside shoulder of the offensive tackle. Secures the C gap and contains the quarterback.

NOSE: Plays 0 technique versus run. Drops **Baker** banjo versus pass.

BUCK: Blitzes through the outside shoulder of the offensive guard and secures the B gap.

WEAK END: Plays 5 technique.

WHIP: Rushes from the edge. Contains the quarterback and weakside run. Chases strongside run.

FREE SAFETY: Lines up as though he's playing cover 2. Drops **Charlie** banjo versus pass. Comes up quickly and helps contain versus weakside run. Checks throwback first and then pursues versus strongside run.

STRONG CORNER: Covers receiver #1. Gives the quarterback a cover 2, pre-snap read. Inside/outside technique is dependent upon field position and the distance of the flanker's split.

WEAK CORNER: Covers receiver #1. Gives the quarterback a cover 2, pre-snap read. Inside/outside technique is dependent upon field position and the distance of the split end's split.

STUNT #51

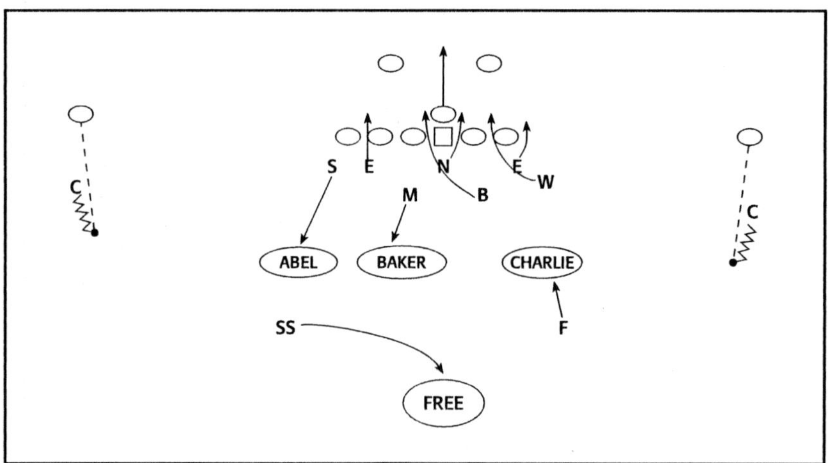

STUNT DESCRIPTION: This banjo blitz features a five-man pass rush.

SECONDARY COVERAGE: Cover 1 disguised as cover 2. Stud, Mike, and the free safety drop off into banjo coverage, and the strong safety is free.

STRONG SAFETY: Lines up as though he's playing cover 2. Drops to centerfield versus pass. Comes up quickly and contains versus strongside run. Checks throwback first and then pursues versus weakside run.

STUD: Plays 9 technique versus run. Drops **Abel** banjo versus pass.

STRONG END: Plays 5 technique versus run. Contains the quarterback versus pass.

MIKE: Plays base technique versus run. Drops **Baker** banjo versus pass.

NOSE: Slants into the weakside A gap.

BUCK: Blitzes through the strongside A gap.

WEAK END: Slants to the C gap. Secures the C gap and contains the quarterback.

WHIP: Blitzes through the B gap.

FREE SAFETY: Lines up as though he's playing cover 2. Versus pass, Drops **Charlie** banjo versus pass. Comes up quickly and helps contain versus weakside run. Checks throwback first, and then pursues versus strongside run..

STRONG CORNER: Covers receiver #1. Gives the quarterback a cover 2, pre-snap read. Inside/outside technique is dependent upon field position and the distance of the flanker's split.

WEAK CORNER: Covers receiver #1. Gives the quarterback a cover 2, pre-snap read. Inside/outside technique is dependent upon field position and the distance of the split end's split.

STUNT #52

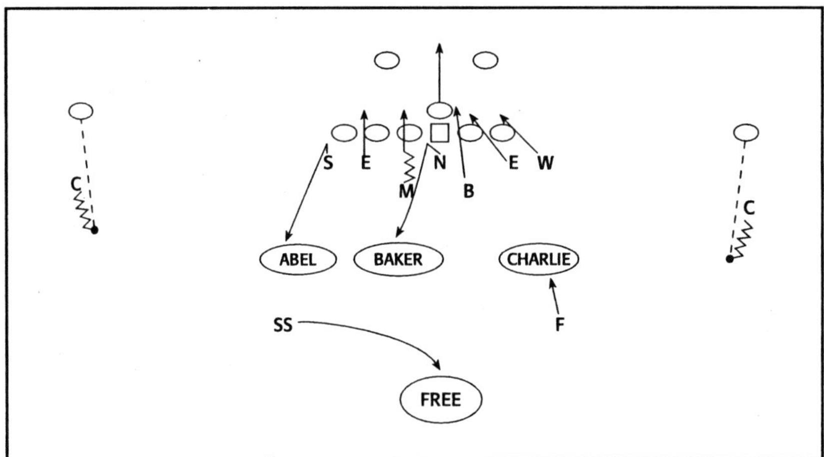

STUNT DESCRIPTION: This banjo blitz gives the **illusion** of a six-man pass rush.

SECONDARY COVERAGE: Cover 1 disguised as cover 2. Stud, nose, and the free safety drop off into banjo coverage, and the strong safety is free.

STRONG SAFETY: Lines up as though he's playing cover 2. Drops to centerfield versus pass. Comes up quickly and contains versus strongside run. Checks throwback first and then pursues versus weakside run.

STUD: Plays 9 technique versus run. Drops **Abel** banjo versus pass.

STRONG END: Plays 5 technique versus run. Contains the quarterback versus pass.

MIKE: Creeps toward the line during cadence. Blitzes through the outside shoulder of the offensive guard and secures the B gap.

NOSE: Slants into the strongside A gap. Secures the A gap versus run, and drops **Baker** banjo versus pass.

BUCK: Blitzes through the weakside A gap.

WEAK END: Slants across the face of the offensive tackle into the B gap.

WHIP: Blitzes through the outside shoulder of the offensive tackle. Secures the C gap and contains the quarterback.

FREE SAFETY: Lines up as though he's playing cover 2. Drops **Charlie** banjo versus pass. Comes up quickly and contains versus weakside run. Checks throwback first, and then pursues versus strongside run.

STRONG CORNER: Covers receiver #1. Gives the quarterback a cover 2, pre-snap read. Inside/outside technique is dependent upon field position and the distance of the flanker's split.

WEAK CORNER: Covers receiver #1. Gives the quarterback a cover 2, pre-snap read. Inside/outside technique is dependent upon field position and the distance of the split end's split.

STUNT #53

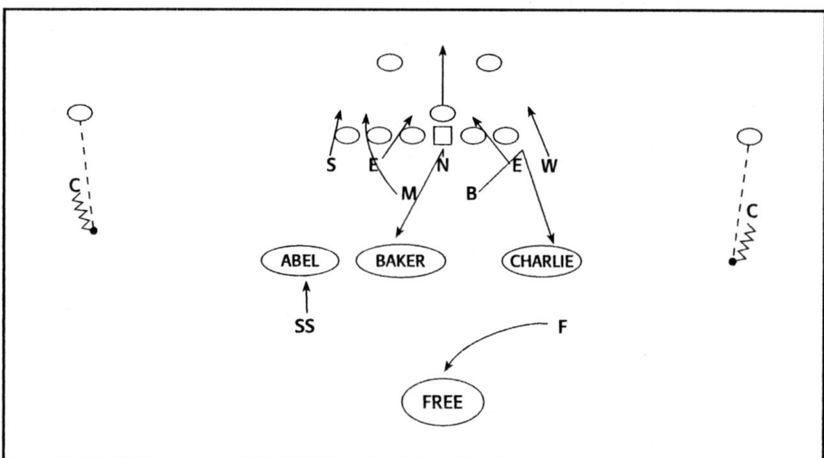

STUNT DESCRIPTION: This banjo blitz gives the **illusion** of a five-man pass rush.

SECONDARY COVERAGE: Cover 1 disguised as cover 2. The strong safety, nose, and Buck drop off into banjo coverage, and the free safety is free.

STRONG SAFETY: Lines up as though he's playing cover 2. Drops **Abel** banjo versus pass.. Comes up quickly and contains versus strongside run. Checks throwback first, and then pursues versus weakside run.

STUD: Plays 9 technique versus run. Contains the quarterback versus pass.

STRONG END: Slants across the offensive tackle's face into the B gap.

MIKE: Blitzes through the outside shoulder of the offensive tackle and secures the C gap.

NOSE: Plays 0 technique versus run. Drops **Baker** banjo versus pass.

BUCK: Fakes a blitz toward the C gap. Secures the C gap versus run and drops **Charlie** banjo versus pass.

WEAK END: Slants across the face of the offensive tackle into the B gap.

WHIP: Rushes from the edge. Contains the quarterback and strongside run. Chases weakside run.

FREE SAFETY: Lines up as though he's playing cover 2. Drops to centerfield versus pass. Comes up quickly and contains versus weakside run. Checks throwback first, and then pursues versus strongside run.

STRONG CORNER: Covers receiver #1. Gives the quarterback a cover 2, pre-snap read. Inside/outside technique is dependent upon field position and the distance of the flanker's split.

WEAK CORNER: Covers receiver #1. Gives the quarterback a cover 2, pre-snap read. Inside/outside technique is dependent upon field position and the distance of the split end's split.

STUNT #54

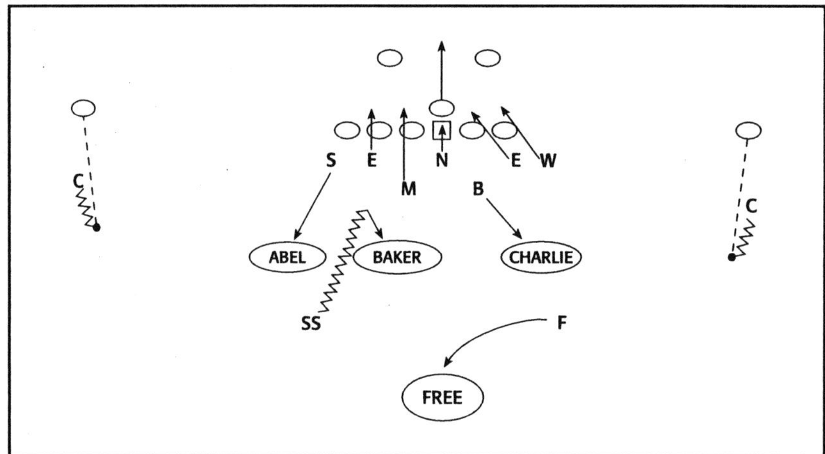

STUNT DESCRIPTION: This banjo blitz features a fake strong-safety blitz and gives the defense a five-man pass rush.

SECONDARY COVERAGE: Cover 1 disguised as cover 2. The strong safety, Stud, and Buck drop off into banjo coverage, and the free safety is free.

STRONG SAFETY: Lines up as though he's playing cover 2. Creeps toward the line during cadence and convinces the quarterback that he intends to blitz inside. Drops **Baker** banjo versus pass. Contains strongside run and checks the tight end before pursuing weakside run.

STUD: Plays 9 technique versus run. Drops **Abel** banjo versus pass.

STRONG END: Plays 5 technique versus run. Contains the quarterback versus pass.

MIKE: Blitzes through the outside shoulder of the offensive guard and secures the B gap.

NOSE: Plays 0 technique.

BUCK: Scrapes outside and contains versus weakside run. Pursues strongside run from an inside-out position. Drops **Charlie** banjo versus pass.

WEAK END: Slants across the face of the offensive tackle into the B gap.

WHIP: Rushes through the outside shoulder of the offensive tackle. Secures the C gap and contains the quarterback.

FREE SAFETY: Lines up as though he's playing cover 2. Drops to centerfield versus pass. Comes up quickly and contains versus weakside run. Checks throwback first, and then pursues versus strongside run.

STRONG CORNER: Covers receiver #1. Gives the quarterback a cover 2, pre-snap read. Inside/outside technique is dependent upon field position and the distance of the flanker's split.

WEAK CORNER: Covers receiver #1. Gives the quarterback a cover 2, pre-snap read. Inside/outside technique is dependent upon field position and the distance of the split end's split.

STUNT #55

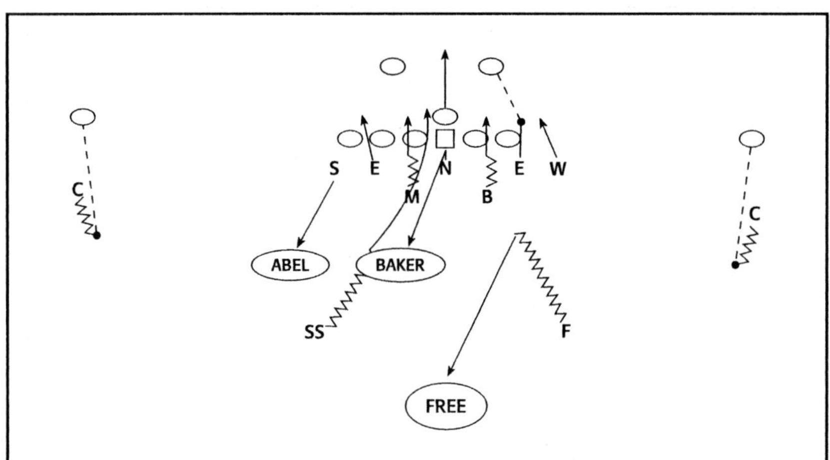

STUNT DESCRIPTION: This gumbo blitz features a strong-safety blitz and gives the defense a five-man pass rush. It also gives the offense the pre-snap read that the defense is "sending the house."

SECONDARY COVERAGE: Cover 1 disguised as cover 2. Stud and nose drop off into gumbo coverage, and the weak end spies the near back. The free safety is free.

STRONG SAFETY: Lines up as though he's playing cover 2. Quickly moves toward the line during cadence and blitzes through the strongside A gap.

STUD: Plays 9 technique versus run. Drops **Abel** gumbo versus pass.

STRONG END: Penetrates the C gap at the snap. Secures the C gap and contains the quarterback.

MIKE: Creeps toward the line during cadence and blitzes through the outside shoulder of the offensive guard at the snap. Secures the B gap.

NOSE: Plays 0 technique versus run. Drops **Baker** gumbo versus pass.

BUCK: Creeps toward the line during cadence and blitzes through the outside shoulder of the offensive guard at the snap. Secures the B gap.

WEAK END: Plays 5 technique versus run. Spies the near back versus pass.

WHIP: Rushes from the edge. Contains the quarterback and strongside run. Chases weakside run.

FREE SAFETY: Lines up as though he's playing cover 2. Creeps toward the line during cadence and convinces the quarterback that a double safety blitz is in progress. Drops to centerfield versus pass. Comes up quickly and contains versus weakside run. Checks throwback first, and then pursues versus strongside run.

STRONG CORNER: Covers receiver #1. Gives the quarterback a cover 2, pre-snap read. Inside/outside technique is dependent upon field position and the distance of the flanker's split.

WEAK CORNER: Covers receiver #1. Gives the quarterback a cover 2, pre-snap read. Inside/outside technique is dependent upon field position and the distance of the split end's split.

STUNT #56

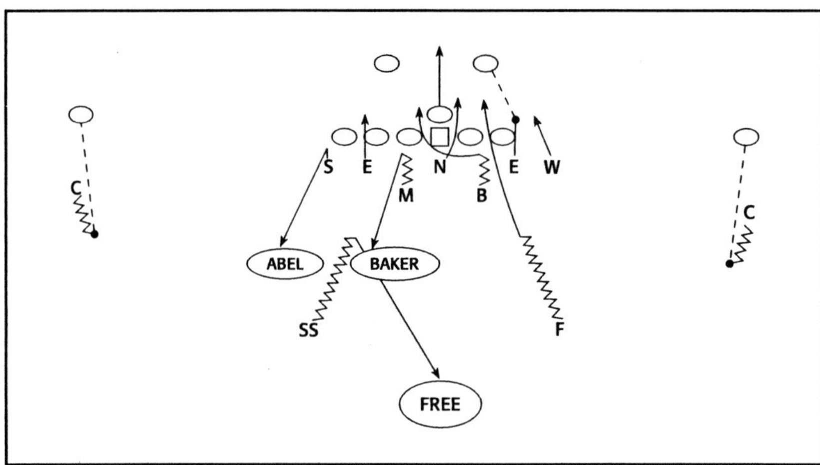

STUNT DESCRIPTION: This gumbo blitz features a weak-safety blitz and gives the quarterback the pre-snap read that the defense is "sending the house."

SECONDARY COVERAGE: Cover 1 disguised as cover 2. Stud and nose drop off into gumbo coverage, and the weak end spies the near back. The strong safety is free.

STRONG SAFETY: Lines up as though he's playing cover 2. Creeps toward the line during cadence and convinces the quarterback that a double-safety blitz is in progress. Drops to centerfield versus pass. Comes up quickly and contains versus strongside run. Checks the tight end before pursuing weakside run.

STUD: Plays 9 technique versus run. Drops **Abel** gumbo versus pass.

STRONG END: Plays 5 technique versus run. Contains the quarterback versus pass.

MIKE: Creeps toward the line during cadence and shows blitz. Secures the B gap versus run and drops **Baker** gumbo versus pass.

NOSE: Slants into the weakside A gap.

BUCK: Creeps toward the line as though he's going to blitz through the outside shoulder of the guard. Blitzes through the strongside A gap as the ball is being snapped.

WEAK END: Plays 5 technique versus run. Spies the near back versus pass.

WHIP: Rushes from the edge. Contains the quarterback and strongside run. Chases weakside run.

FREE SAFETY: Lines up as though he's playing cover 2. Quickly moves toward the line during cadence and blitzes through the weakside B gap.

STRONG CORNER: Covers receiver #1. Gives the quarterback a cover 2, pre-snap read. Inside/outside technique is dependent upon field position and the distance of the flanker's split.

WEAK CORNER: Covers receiver #1. Gives the quarterback a cover 2, pre-snap read. Inside/outside technique is dependent upon field position and the distance of the split end's split.

STUNT #57

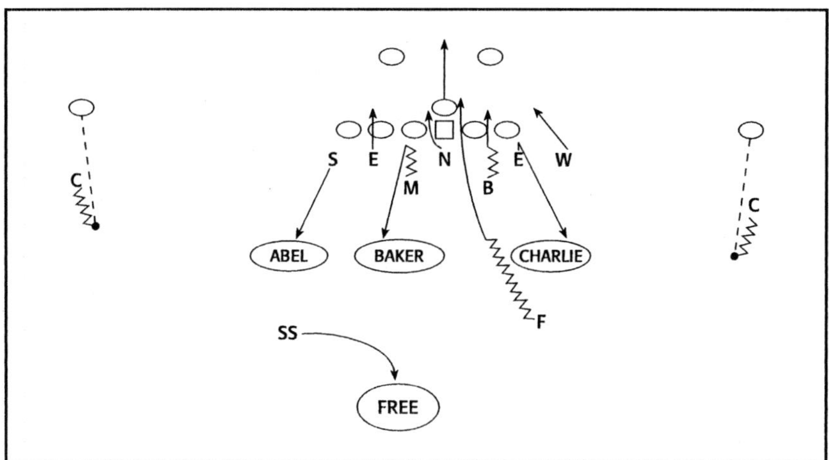

STUNT DESCRIPTION: This banjo blitz features a free-safety blitz

SECONDARY COVERAGE: Cover 1 disguised as cover 2. Stud, Mike, and the weak end drop off into banjo coverage, and the strong safety is free.

STRONG SAFETY: Lines up as though he's playing cover 2. Drops to centerfield versus pass. Comes up quickly and contains versus strongside run. Checks the tight end before pursuing weakside run.

STUD: Plays 9 technique versus run. Drops **Abel** banjo versus pass.

STRONG END: Plays 5 technique versus run. Contains the quarterback versus pass.

MIKE: Creeps toward the line during cadence and shows blitz. Secures the B gap versus run and drops **Baker** banjo versus pass.

NOSE: Slants into the strongside A gap.

BUCK: Creeps toward the line and blitzes through the outside shoulder of the guard. Secures the B gap.

WEAK END: Plays 5 technique versus run. Drops **Charlie** banjo versus pass.

WHIP: Rushes from the edge. Contains the quarterback and strongside run. Chases weakside run.

FREE SAFETY: Lines up as though he's playing cover 2. Quickly moves toward the line during cadence and blitzes through the weakside A gap.

STRONG CORNER: Covers receiver #1. Gives the quarterback a cover 2, pre-snap read. Inside/outside technique is dependent upon field position and the distance of the flanker's split.

WEAK CORNER: Covers receiver #1. Gives the quarterback a cover 2, pre-snap read. Inside/outside technique is dependent upon field position and the distance of the split end's split.

STUNT #58

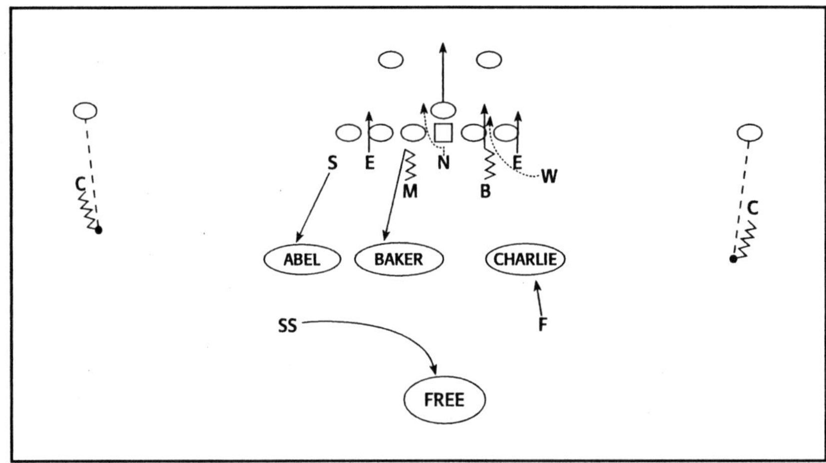

STUNT DESCRIPTION: This banjo blitz features a delayed twin stunt through the weakside B gap.

SECONDARY COVERAGE: Cover 1 disguised as cover 2. Stud, Mike, and the free safety drop off into banjo coverage, and the strong safety is free.

STRONG SAFETY: Lines up as though he's playing cover 2. Drops to centerfield versus pass. Comes up quickly and contains versus strongside run. Checks the tight end before pursuing weakside run.

STUD: Plays 9 technique versus run. Drops **Abel** banjo versus pass.

STRONG END: Plays 5 technique versus run. Contains the quarterback versus pass.

MIKE: Creeps toward the line during cadence and shows blitz. Secures the B gap versus run and drops **Baker** banjo versus pass.

NOSE: Plays 0 technique versus run. Delay rushes through the strongside A gap (after engaging the center's block) versus pass.

BUCK: Creeps toward the line and blitzes through the outside shoulder of the guard. Secures the B gap.

WEAK END: Plays 5 technique versus run. Contains the quarterback versus pass.

WHIP: Cheats back slightly. Plays 9 technique versus run. Delay blitzes (twin stunt) through the weakside B gap versus pass.

FREE SAFETY: Lines up as though he's playing cover 2. Drops **Charlie** banjo versus dropback pass. Comes up quickly and contains versus weakside run. Checks throwback before pursuing strongside run.

STRONG CORNER: Covers receiver #1. Gives the quarterback a cover 2, pre-snap read. Inside/outside technique is dependent upon field position and the distance of the flanker's split.

WEAK CORNER: Covers receiver #1. Gives the quarterback a cover 2, pre-snap read. Inside/outside technique is dependent upon field position and the distance of the split end's split.

STUNT #59

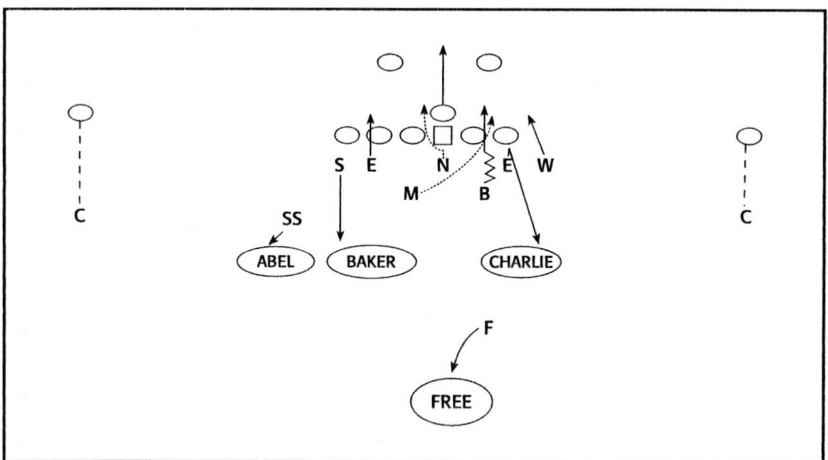

STUNT DESCRIPTION: This banjo blitz features a delayed twin stunt through the weakside B gap.

SECONDARY COVERAGE: Cover 1 disguised as cover 3. The strong safety, Stud, and the weak end drop off into banjo coverage, and the free safety is free.

STRONG SAFETY: Lines up as though he's playing cover 3. Keys the tight end. If he blocks, the strong safety comes up quickly and contains. If he releases, the strong safety drops **Abel** banjo. Checks the tight end before pursuing weakside run.

STUD: Plays 9 technique versus run. Drops **Baker** banjo versus pass.

STRONG END: Plays 5 technique versus run. Contains the quarterback versus pass.

MIKE: Plays base technique versus run. Delay blitzes through the weakside B gap (twin stunt) versus pass.

NOSE: Plays 0 technique versus run. Delay rushes through the strongside A gap (after engaging the center's block) versus pass.

BUCK: Creeps toward the line and blitzes through the outside shoulder of the guard. Secures the B gap.

WEAK END: Plays 5 technique versus run. Drops **Charlie** banjo versus pass.

WHIP: Rushes from the edge. Contains the quarterback and strongside run. Chases weakside run.

FREE SAFETY: Free versus pass. Provides alley support versus run.

STRONG CORNER: Covers receiver #1. Inside/outside technique is dependent upon field position and the distance of the flanker's split.

WEAK CORNER: Covers receiver #1. Inside/outside technique is dependent upon field position and the distance of the split end's split.

STUNT #60

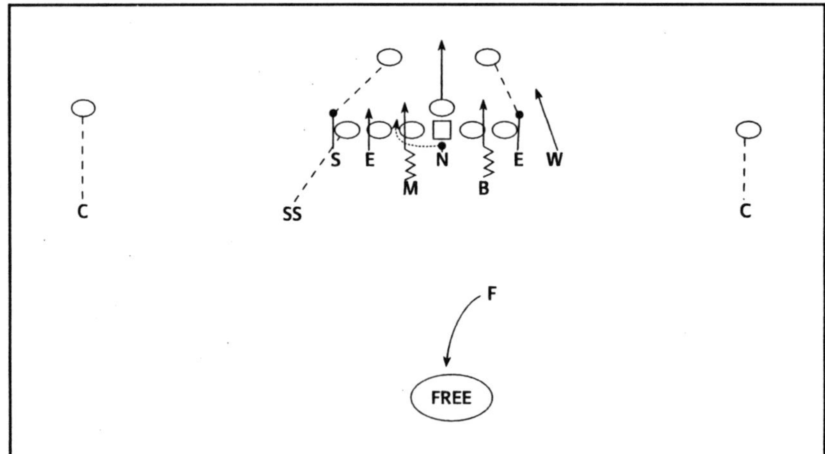

STUNT DESCRIPTION: This stunt gives the offense the **illusion** of a seven-man pass rush and features a delayed twin stunt by the nose.

SECONDARY COVERAGE: Cover 1 disguised as cover 3. Stud and the weak end spy the running backs. The strong safety covers the tight end, and the free safety is free.

STRONG SAFETY: Lines up as though he's playing cover 3. Keys the tight end. If he blocks, the strong safety comes up quickly and contains. If he releases, the strong safety covers him.

STUD: Plays 9 technique versus run. Spies the near back versus pass.

STRONG END: Plays 5 technique versus run. Contains the quarterback versus pass.

MIKE: Creeps toward the line during cadence and blitzes through the outside shoulder of the offensive guard.

NOSE: Plays 0 technique versus run. Delay rushes through the strongside B gap (twin stunt) versus pass.

BUCK: Creeps toward the line and blitzes through the outside shoulder of the guard. Secures the B gap.

WEAK END: Plays 5 technique versus run. Spies the near back versus pass.

WHIP: Rushes from the edge. Contains the quarterback and strongside run. Chases weakside run.

FREE SAFETY: Free versus pass. Provides alley support versus pass.

STRONG CORNER: Covers receiver #1. Inside/outside technique is dependent upon field position and the distance of the flanker's split.

WEAK CORNER: Covers receiver #1. Inside/outside technique is dependent upon field position and the distance of the split end's split.

STUNT #61

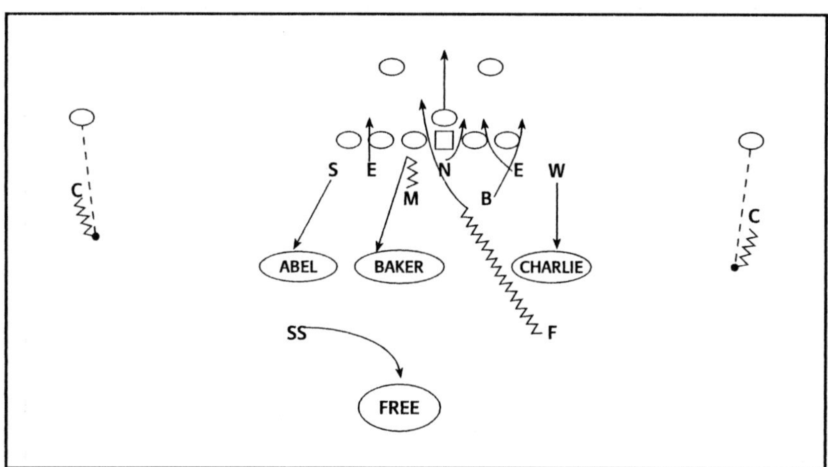

STUNT DESCRIPTION: This banjo blitz features a free-safety blitz.

SECONDARY COVERAGE: Cover 1 disguised as cover 2. Stud, Mike, and Whip drop off into banjo coverage, and the strong safety is free.

STRONG SAFETY: Lines up as though he's playing cover 2. Drops to centerfield versus pass. Comes up quickly and contains versus strongside run. Checks the tight end before pursuing weakside run.

STUD: Plays 9 technique versus run. Drops **Abel** banjo versus pass.

STRONG END: Plays 5 technique versus run. Contains the quarterback versus pass.

MIKE: Creeps toward the line during cadence and shows blitz. Secures the B gap versus run and drops **Baker** banjo versus pass.

NOSE: Slants into the weakside A gap.

BUCK: Blitzes through the outside shoulder of the offensive tackle and secures the C gap. Contains the quarterback versus pass.

WEAK END: Slants across the offensive tackle's face into the B gap.

WHIP: Plays 9 technique versus run. Drops **Charlie** banjo versus pass.

FREE SAFETY: Lines up as though he's playing cover 2. Quickly moves toward the line during cadence and blitzes through the strongside A gap.

STRONG CORNER: Covers receiver #1. Gives the quarterback a cover 2, pre-snap read. Inside/outside technique is dependent upon field position and the distance of the flanker's split.

WEAK CORNER: Covers receiver #1. Gives the quarterback a cover 2, pre-snap read. Inside/outside technique is dependent upon field position and the distance of the split end's split.

STUNT #62

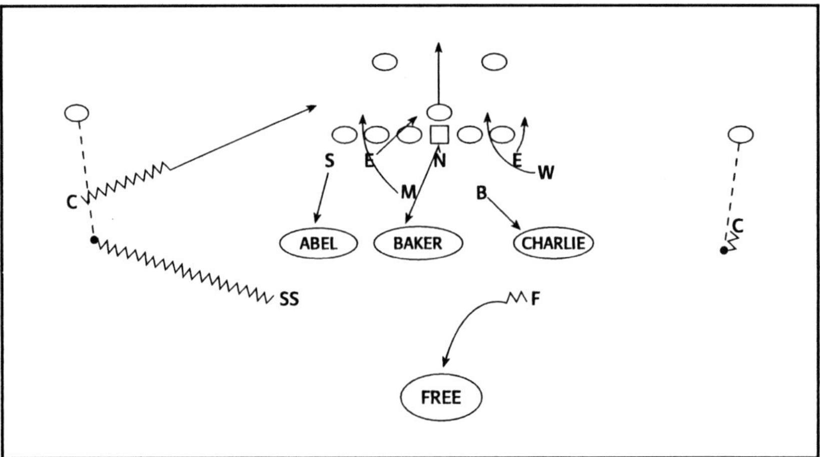

STUNT DESCRIPTION: This banjo blitz features a strong-cornerback blitz.

SECONDARY COVERAGE: Cover 1 disguised as cover 2. Stud, nose, and Buck drop off into banjo coverage, and the free safety is free.

STRONG SAFETY: Lines up as though he's playing cover 2. Moves to a position during cadence that enables him to cover the flanker.

STUD: Plays 9 technique versus run. Drops **Abel** banjo versus pass.

STRONG END: Slants across the offensive tackle's face into the B gap.

MIKE: Blitzes through the outside shoulder of the offensive tackle, secures the C gap, and contains the quarterback.

NOSE: Plays 0 technique versus run. Drops **Baker** banjo versus pass.

BUCK: Scrapes outside and contains versus weakside run. Pursues strongside run from an inside-out position. Drops **Charlie** banjo versus pass.

WEAK END: Slants into the C gap. Secures the C gap and contains the quarterback.

WHIP: Cheats back slightly and blitzes through the B gap.

FREE SAFETY: Gives the quarterback a cover 2 pre-snap read. Plays centerfield versus pass, and provides alley support versus run.

STRONG CORNER: Gives the quarterback a cover 2, pre-snap read. Creeps inside during cadence and rushes from the edge. Contains the quarterback and strongside run. Chases weakside run.

WEAK CORNER: Covers receiver #1. Gives the quarterback a cover 2, pre-snap read. Inside/ outside technique is dependent upon field position and the distance of the split end's split.

STUNT #63

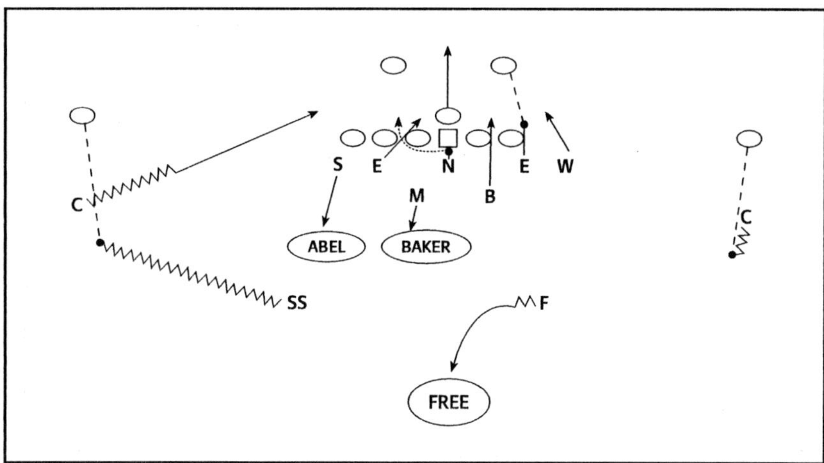

STUNT DESCRIPTION: This gumbo blitz features a strong-cornerback blitz and a twin stunt through the strongside B gap.

SECONDARY COVERAGE: Cover 1 disguised as cover 2. Stud and Mike drop off into gumbo coverage, and the weak end spies his near back. The free safety is free.

STRONG SAFETY: Lines up as though he's playing cover 2. Moves to a position during cadence that enables him to cover the flanker.

STUD: Plays 9 technique versus run. Drops **Abel** gumbo versus pass.

STRONG END: Slants across the offensive tackle's face into the B gap.

MIKE: Scrapes into the C gap versus strongside run. Pursues weakside run from an inside-out position. Drops **Baker** gumbo versus pass.

NOSE: Plays 0 technique versus run. Delay rushes (twin stunt) through the strongside B gap versus pass.

BUCK: Blitzes through the outside shoulder of the offensive guard and secures the B gap.

WEAK END: Plays 5 technique versus run. Spies the near back versus pass.

WHIP: Rushes from the edge. Contains the quarterback and weakside run. Chases strongside run.

FREE SAFETY: Gives the quarterback a cover 2, pre-snap read. Plays centerfield versus pass, and provides alley support versus run.

STRONG CORNER: Gives the quarterback a cover 2, pre-snap read. Creeps inside during cadence and rushes from the edge. Contains the quarterback and strongside run. Chases weakside run.

WEAK CORNER: Covers receiver #1. Gives the quarterback a cover 2, pre-snap read. Inside/outside technique is dependent upon field position and the distance of the split end's split.

STUNT #64

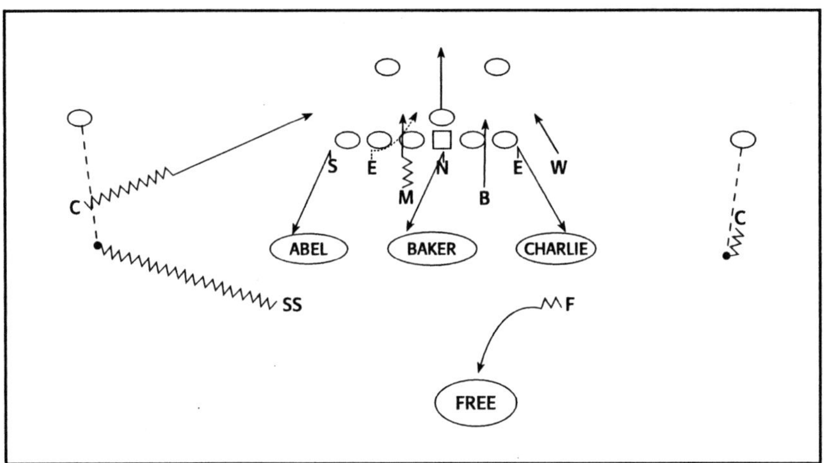

STUNT DESCRIPTION: This banjo blitz features a strong-cornerback blitz and a twin stunt through the strongside B gap.

SECONDARY COVERAGE: Cover 1 disguised as cover 2. Stud, nose, and the weak end drop off into banjo coverage, and the free safety is free.

STRONG SAFETY: Lines up as though he's playing cover 2. Moves to a position during cadence that enables him to cover the flanker.

STUD: Plays 9 technique versus run. Drops **Abel** banjo versus pass.

STRONG END: Plays 5 technique versus run. Slants behind Mike through the B gap versus pass.

MIKE: Creeps toward the line during cadence and blitzes through the outside shoulder of the offensive guard.

NOSE: Plays 0 technique versus run. Drops **Baker** banjo versus pass.

BUCK: Blitzes through the outside shoulder of the offensive guard and secures the B gap.

WEAK END: Plays 5 technique versus run. Drops **Charlie** banjo versus pass.

WHIP: Rushes from the edge. Contains the quarterback and weakside run. Chases strongside run.

FREE SAFETY: Gives the quarterback a cover 2, pre-snap read. Plays centerfield versus pass, and provides alley support versus run.

STRONG CORNER: Gives the quarterback a cover 2, pre-snap read. Creeps inside during cadence and rushes from the edge. Contains the quarterback and strongside run. Chases weakside run.

WEAK CORNER: Covers receiver #1. Gives the quarterback a cover 2, pre-snap read. Inside/ outside technique is dependent upon field position and the distance of the split end's split.

STUNT #65

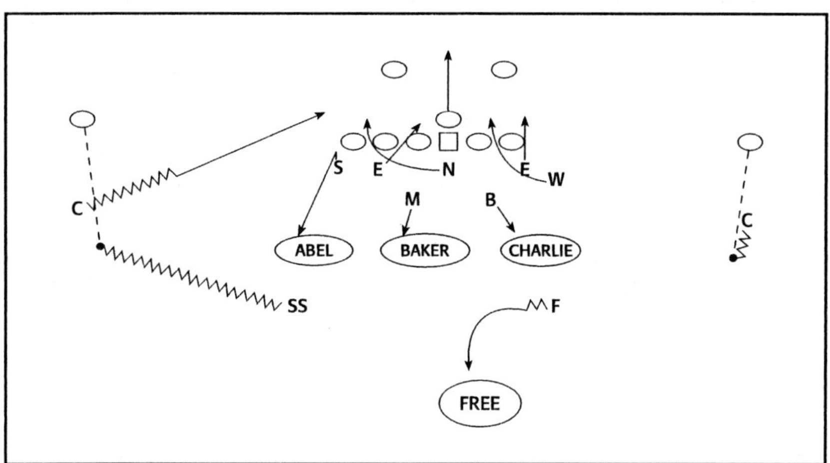

STUNT DESCRIPTION: This banjo blitz features a strong-cornerback blitz.

SECONDARY COVERAGE: Cover 1 disguised as cover 2. Stud, Mike, and Buck drop off into banjo coverage, and the free safety is free.

STRONG SAFETY: Lines up as though he's playing cover 2. Moves to a position during cadence that enables him to cover the flanker.

STUD: Plays 9 technique versus run. Drops **Abel** banjo versus pass.

STRONG END: Slants across the offensive tackle's face into the B gap.

MIKE: Pursues strongside run from an inside-out position. Secures the strongside A gap before pursuing weakside run. Drops **Baker** banjo versus pass.

NOSE: Loops across the offensive tackle's face into the strongside C gap.

BUCK: Scrapes outside and contains versus weakside run. Checks the strongside A gap as he pursues strongside run. Drops **Charlie** banjo versus pass.

WEAK END: Plays 5 technique versus run. Contains the quarterback versus pass.

WHIP: Cheats back slightly and blitzes through the B gap.

FREE SAFETY: Gives the quarterback a cover 2, pre-snap read. Plays centerfield versus pass, and provides alley support versus run.

STRONG CORNER: Gives the quarterback a cover 2, pre-snap read. Creeps inside during cadence and rushes from the edge. Contains the quarterback and strongside run. Chases weakside run.

WEAK CORNER: Covers receiver #1. Gives the quarterback a cover 2, pre-snap read. Inside/outside technique is dependent upon field position and the distance of the split end's split.

STUNT #66

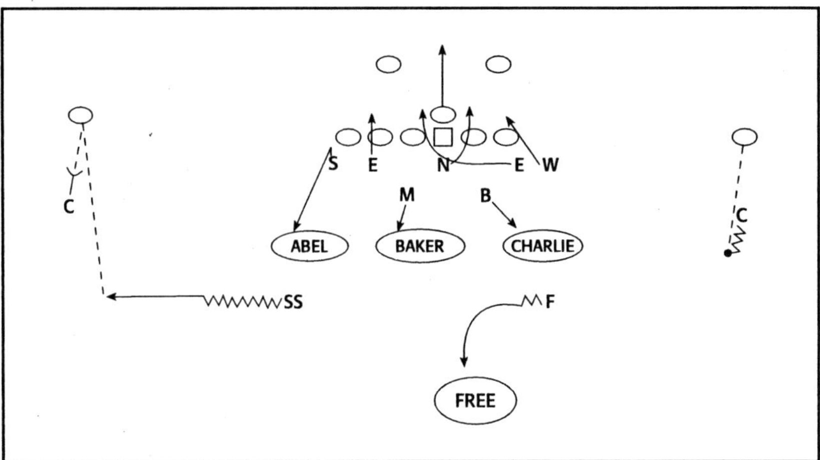

STUNT DESCRIPTION: This banjo blitz features double coverage on the flanker.

SECONDARY COVERAGE: Cover 1 disguised as cover 2. Stud, Mike, and Buck drop off into banjo coverage, and the free safety is free. Both the cornerback and the strong safety double cover the flanker.

STRONG SAFETY: Lines up in a cover 2 technique. Moves to a position during cadence that enables him to cover the flanker's deep routes.

STUD: Plays 9 technique versus run. Drops **Abel** banjo versus pass.

STRONG END: Plays 5 technique versus run. Contains the quarterback versus pass.

MIKE: Plays base technique versus run. Drops **Baker** banjo versus pass.

NOSE: Rips through the inside shoulder of the guard and controls the weakside A gap.

BUCK: Scrapes outside and contains versus weakside run. Pursues strongside run from an inside-out position. Drops **Charlie** banjo versus pass.

WEAK END: Loops across the face of the center into the strongside A gap.

WHIP: Rushes through the outside shoulder of the offensive tackle. Secures the C gap and contains the quarterback.

FREE SAFETY: Gives the quarterback a cover 2, pre-snap read. Plays centerfield versus pass, and provides alley support versus run.

STRONG CORNER: Gives the quarterback a cover 2, pre-snap read. Jams the flanker and tries to funnel him inside while covering him man-to-man.

WEAK CORNER: Covers receiver #1. Gives the quarterback a cover 2, pre-snap read. Inside/outside technique is dependent upon field position and the distance of the split end's split.

STUNT #67

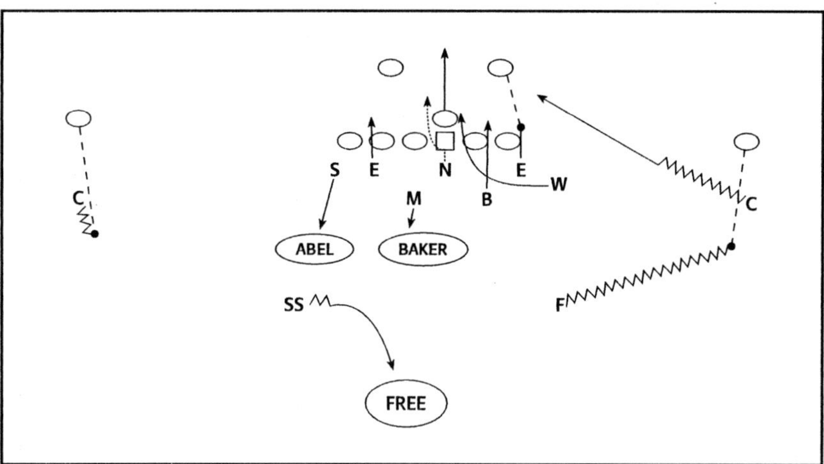

STUNT DESCRIPTION: This gumbo blitz features a weak-cornerback blitz.

SECONDARY COVERAGE: Cover 1 disguised as cover 2. Stud and Mike drop off into gumbo coverage, and the weak end spies the near back. The strong safety is free.

STRONG SAFETY: Gives the quarterback a cover 2, pre-snap read. Moves to a position during cadence that enables him to play centerfield versus pass, and provide alley support versus run.

STUD: Plays 9 technique versus run. Drops **Abel** gumbo versus pass.

STRONG END: Plays 5 technique versus run. Contains the quarterback versus pass.

MIKE: Plays base technique versus run. Drops **Baker** banjo versus pass.

NOSE: Plays 0 technique versus run. Rushes to the strongside A gap after engaging the center's block versus pass.

BUCK: Blitzes through the outside shoulder of the offensive guard and controls the B gap.

WEAK END: Plays 5 technique versus run. Spies the near back versus pass.

WHIP: Cheats back slightly and blitzes through the weakside A gap.

FREE SAFETY: Gives the quarterback a cover 2, pre-snap read. Moves to a position during cadence that enables him to cover the split end.

STRONG CORNER: Covers receiver #1. Gives the quarterback a cover 2, pre-snap read. Inside/outside technique is dependent upon field position and the distance of the flanker's split.

WEAK CORNER: Gives the quarterback a cover 2, pre-snap read. Creeps inside during cadence and blitzes hard from the edge. Contains the quarterback and weakside run. Chases strongside run.

STUNT #68

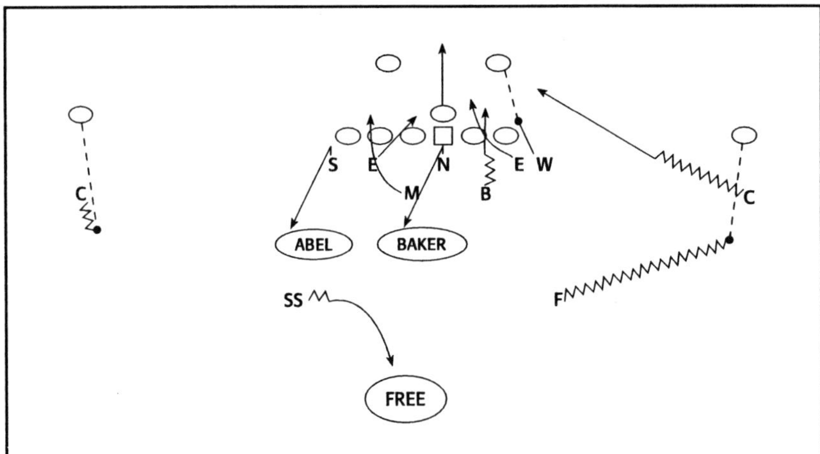

STUNT DESCRIPTION: This gumbo blitz features a weak-cornerback blitz and a twin stunt through the weakside B gap.

SECONDARY COVERAGE: Cover 1 disguised as cover 2. Stud and nose drop off into gumbo coverage, and Whip spies the near back. The strong safety is free.

STRONG SAFETY: Gives the quarterback a cover 2, pre-snap read. Moves to a position during cadence that enables him to play centerfield versus pass, and provide alley support versus run.

STUD: Plays 9 technique versus run. Drops **Abel** gumbo versus pass.

STRONG END: Slants across the offensive tackle's face into the B gap.

MIKE: Blitzes through the outside shoulder of the offensive tackle. Secures the C gap and contains the quarterback.

NOSE: Plays 0 technique versus run. Drops **Baker** gumbo versus pass.

BUCK: Creeps toward the line during cadence and blitzes through the outside shoulder of the offensive guard.

WEAK END: Slants behind Buck through the B gap (twin stunt).

WHIP: Slants to the outside shoulder of the offensive tackle. Secures the C gap and spies the near back.

FREE SAFETY: Gives the quarterback a cover 2, pre-snap read. Moves to a position during cadence that enables him to cover the split end.

STRONG CORNER: Covers receiver #1. Gives the quarterback a cover 2, pre-snap read. Inside/outside technique is dependent upon field position and the distance of the flanker's split.

WEAK CORNER: Gives the quarterback a cover 2, pre-snap read. Creeps inside during cadence and blitzes hard from the edge. Contains the quarterback and weakside run. Chases strongside run.

STUNT #69

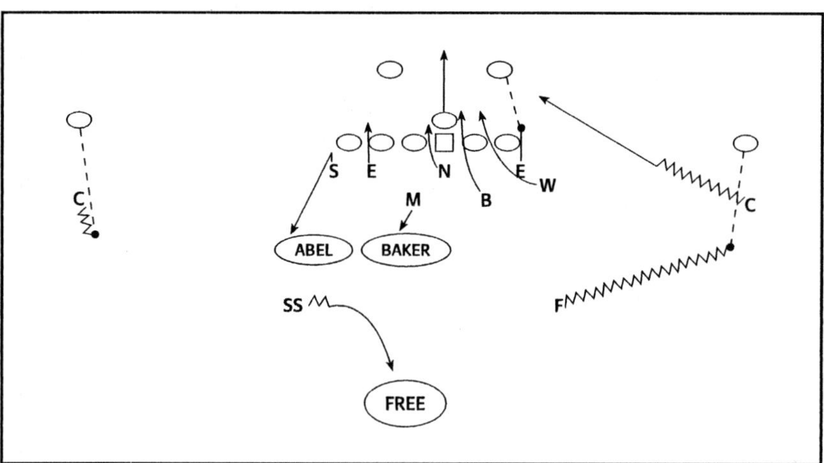

STUNT DESCRIPTION: This gumbo blitz features a weak-cornerback blitz.

SECONDARY COVERAGE: Cover 1 disguised as cover 2. Stud and Mike drop off into gumbo coverage, and the weak end spies the near back. The strong safety is free.

STRONG SAFETY: Gives the quarterback a cover 2, pre-snap read. Moves to a position during cadence that enables him to play centerfield versus pass, and provide alley support versus run.

STUD: Plays 9 technique versus run. Drops **Abel** gumbo versus pass.

STRONG END: Plays 5 technique versus run. Contains the quarterback versus pass.

MIKE: Plays base technique versus run. Drops **Baker** gumbo versus pass.

NOSE: Slants into the strongside A gap.

BUCK: Blitzes through the weakside A gap.

WEAK END: Plays 5 technique versus run. Spies the near back versus pass.

WHIP: Cheats back slightly and blitzes through the B gap.

FREE SAFETY: Gives the quarterback a cover 2, pre-snap read but moves to a position during cadence that enables him to cover the split end.

STRONG CORNER: Covers receiver #1. Gives the quarterback a cover 2, pre-snap read. Inside/outside technique is dependent upon field position and the distance of the flanker's split.

WEAK CORNER: Gives the quarterback a cover 2, pre-snap read. Creeps inside during cadence and blitzes hard from the edge. Contains the quarterback and weakside run. Chases strongside run.

STUNT #70

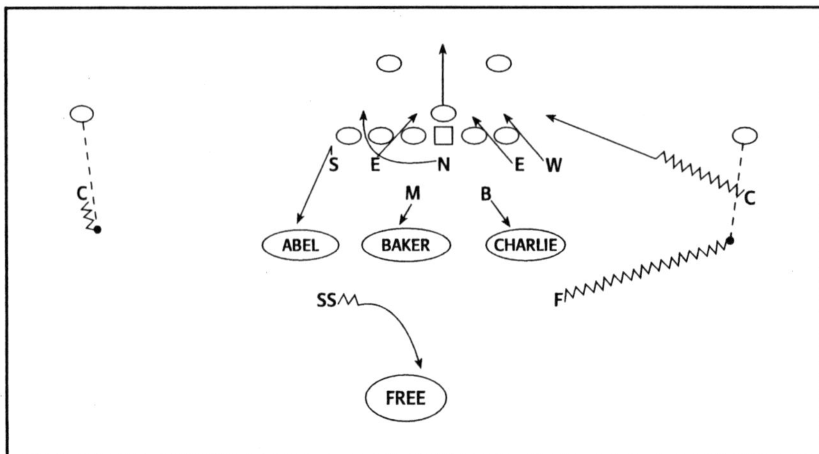

STUNT DESCRIPTION: This banjo blitz features a weak-cornerback blitz.

SECONDARY COVERAGE: Cover 1 disguised as cover 2. Stud, Mike, and Buck drop off into banjo coverage, and the strong safety is free.

STRONG SAFETY: Gives the quarterback a cover 2, pre-snap read. Moves to a position during cadence that enables him to play centerfield versus pass, and provide alley support versus run.

STUD: Plays 9 technique versus run. Drops **Abel** banjo versus pass.

STRONG END: Slants across the face of the offensive tackle into the B gap.

MIKE: Pursues strongside run from an inside-out position and checks both A gaps as he pursues weakside run. Drops **Baker** banjo versus pass.

NOSE: Loops across the face of the offensive tackle into the strongside C gap. Controls the C gap versus run and contains the quarterback versus pass.

BUCK: Pursues strongside and weakside run from an inside-out position. Drops **Charlie** banjo versus pass.

WEAK END: Slants across the offensive tackle's face into the B gap.

WHIP: Rushes through the outside shoulder of the offensive tackle and controls the C gap.

FREE SAFETY: Gives the quarterback a cover 2, pre-snap read but moves to a position during cadence that enables him to cover the split end.

STRONG CORNER: Covers receiver #1. Gives the quarterback a cover 2, pre-snap read. Inside/outside technique is dependent upon field position and the distance of the flanker's split.

WEAK CORNER: Gives the quarterback a cover 2, pre-snap read. Creeps inside during cadence and blitzes hard from the edge. Contains the quarterback and weakside run. Chases strongside run.

STUNT #71

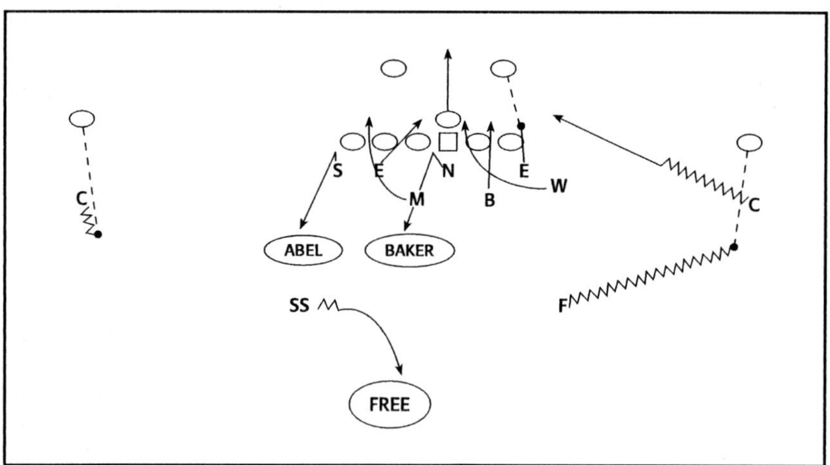

STUNT DESCRIPTION: This gumbo blitz gives the **illusion** of an eight-man pass rush.

SECONDARY COVERAGE: Cover 1 disguised as cover 2. Stud and Buck drop off into gumbo coverage, the weak end spies the near back, and the strong safety is free.

STRONG SAFETY: Gives the quarterback a cover 2, pre-snap read. Moves to a position during cadence that enables him to play centerfield versus pass, and provide alley support versus run.

STUD: Plays 9 technique versus run. Drops **Abel** gumbo versus pass.

STRONG END: Slants into the B gap.

MIKE: Blitzes through the outside shoulder of the offensive tackle, secures the C gap, and contains the quarterback.

NOSE: Slants into the strongside A gap. Secures the A gap versus run and drops **Baker** gumbo versus pass.

BUCK: Blitzes through the B gap.

WEAK END: Plays 5 technique versus run. Spies the near back versus pass.

WHIP: Cheats back slightly and blitzes through the weakside A gap.

FREE SAFETY: Gives the quarterback a cover 2, pre-snap read but moves to a position during cadence that enables him to cover the split end.

STRONG CORNER: Covers receiver #1. Gives the quarterback a cover 2, pre-snap read. Inside/outside technique is dependent upon field position and the distance of the flanker's split.

WEAK CORNER: Gives the quarterback a cover 2, pre-snap read. Creeps inside during cadence and blitzes hard from the edge. Contains the quarterback and weakside run. Chases strongside run.

STUNT #72

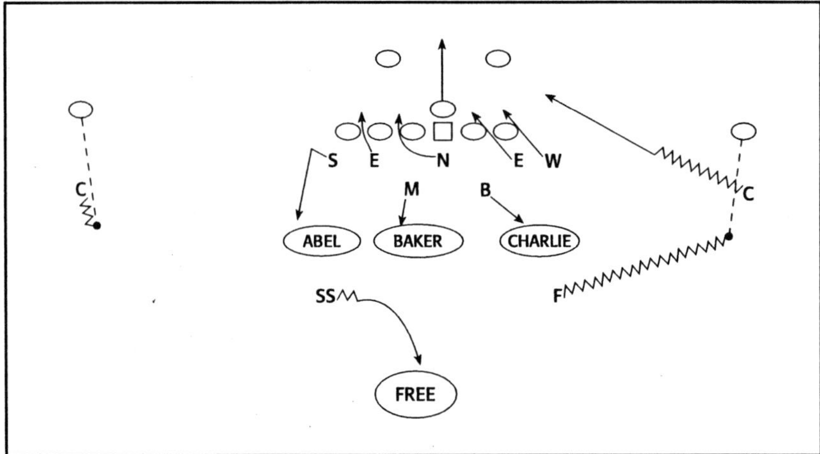

STUNT DESCRIPTION: This banjo blitz slants the defense toward the strongside and blitzes a cornerback toward the weakside.

SECONDARY COVERAGE: Cover 1 disguised as cover 2. Stud, Mike, and Buck drop off into banjo coverage, and the strong safety is free.

STRONG SAFETY: Gives the quarterback a cover 2, pre-snap read. Moves to a position during cadence that enables him to play centerfield versus pass, and provide alley support versus run.

STUD: Slants outside and secures the D gap versus run. Drops **Abel** banjo versus pass.

STRONG END: Penetrates and controls the C gap. Contains the quarterback versus pass.

MIKE: Pursues strongside run from an inside-out position. Checks the weakside A gap as he pursues weakside run. Drops **Baker** banjo versus pass.

NOSE: Slants across the face of the offensive guard into the strongside B gap.

BUCK: Scrapes outside and assists in containment versus weakside run. Checks the weakside A gap as he pursues strongside run. Drops **Charlie** banjo versus pass.

WEAK END: Slants across the offensive tackle's face into the B gap.

WHIP: Rushes through the outside shoulder of the offensive tackle and secures the C gap.

FREE SAFETY: Gives the quarterback a cover 2, pre-snap read but moves to a position during cadence that enables him to cover the split end.

STRONG CORNER: Covers receiver #1. Gives the quarterback a cover 2, pre-snap read. Inside/outside technique is dependent upon field position and the distance of the flanker's split.

WEAK CORNER: Gives the quarterback a cover 2, pre-snap read. Creeps inside during cadence and blitzes hard from the edge. Contains the quarterback and weakside run. Chases strongside run.

STUNT #73

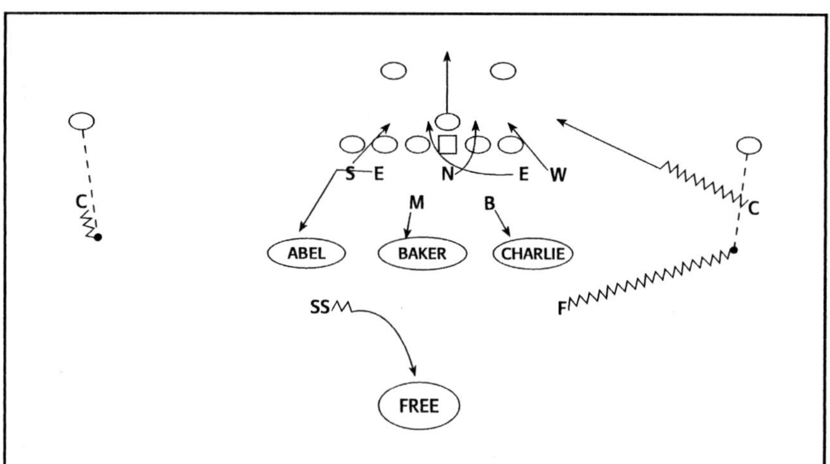

STUNT DESCRIPTION: This banjo blitz provides the defense with a weak-cornerback blitz and a five-man pass rush that is enhanced by line twists.

SECONDARY COVERAGE: Cover 1 disguised as cover 2. The strong end, Mike, and Buck drop off into banjo coverage, and the strong safety is free.

STRONG SAFETY: Gives the quarterback a cover 2, pre-snap read. Moves to a position during cadence that enables him to play centerfield versus pass, and provide alley support versus run.

STUD: Slants across the face of the tight end into the C gap. Controls the C gap versus run and contains the quarterback versus pass.

STRONG END: Loops across the face of the tight end into the D gap. Secures the D gap versus run and drops **Abel** banjo versus pass.

MIKE: Plays base technique versus run. Drops **Baker** banjo versus pass.

NOSE: Slants through the inside shoulder of the guard and secures the weakside A gap.

BUCK: Plays base technique versus run. Drops **Charlie** banjo versus pass.

WEAK END: Loops across the face of the center into the strongside A gap.

WHIP: Rushes through the outside shoulder of the offensive tackle and secures the C gap.

FREE SAFETY: Gives the quarterback a cover 2, pre-snap read but moves to a position during cadence that enables him to cover the split end.

STRONG CORNER: Covers receiver #1. Gives the quarterback a cover 2, pre-snap read. Inside/outside technique is dependent upon field position and the distance of the flanker's split.

WEAK CORNER: Gives the quarterback a cover 2, pre-snap read. Creeps inside during cadence and blitzes hard from the edge. Contains the quarterback and weakside run. Chases strongside run.

STUNT #74

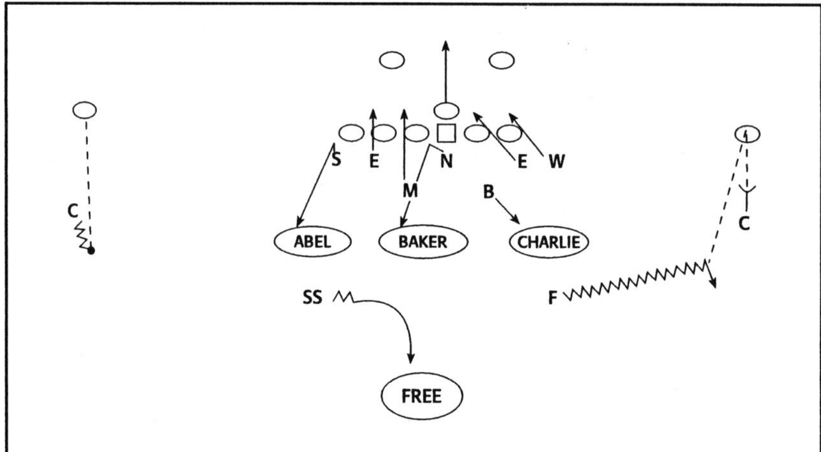

STUNT DESCRIPTION: This banjo blitz provides the defense with a five-man pass rush and double coverage on the split end.

SECONDARY COVERAGE: Cover 1 disguised as cover 2. Stud, Mike, and Buck drop off into banjo coverage, and the strong safety is free.

STRONG SAFETY: Gives the quarterback a cover 2, pre-snap read. Moves to a position during cadence that enables him to play centerfield versus pass, and provide alley support versus run.

STUD: Plays 9 technique versus run. Drops **Abel** banjo versus pass.

STRONG END: Plays 5 technique versus run. Contains the quarterback versus pass.

MIKE: Blitzes through the outside shoulder of the offensive guard and secures the B gap.

NOSE: Slants into and secures the strongside A gap versus run. Drops **Baker** banjo versus pass.

BUCK: Scrapes outside and contains versus weakside run. Checks the weakside A gap as he pursues strongside run from an inside-out position. Drops **Charlie** banjo versus pass.

WEAK END: Slants across the face of the offensive tackle into the B gap.

WHIP: Rushes through the outside shoulder of the offensive tackle and secures the C gap.

FREE SAFETY: Gives the quarterback a cover 2, pre-snap read, but moves to a position during cadence that enables him to cover the split end's deep patterns.

STRONG CORNER: Covers receiver #1. Gives the quarterback a cover 2, pre-snap read. Inside/outside technique is dependent upon field position and the distance of the flanker's split.

WEAK CORNER: Gives the quarterback a cover 2, pre-snap read. Jams the split end and funnels him inside while covering him man-to-man.

CHAPTER 5

COVER 2 STUNTS

STUNTS THAT ENHANCE TWO-MAN COVERAGE

When two-man coverage is employed, both cornerbacks jam the two wide receivers and funnel them to the outside (some coaches may prefer to funnel tightly aligned receivers to the inside). The two safeties use the hashes as landmarks to defend the deep halves of the field. A wide variety of stunt tactics may be employed with this coverage.

Two-Man Techniques for Cornerbacks

A defensive cornerback should:

- Line up so that his inside foot is splitting the receiver's stance.
- Set up with a narrow base, feet parallel, and shoulders square to the line. His weight should be equally balanced on the balls of his feet.
- Focus his concentration on the receiver's midsection.
- Mirror the receiver's release by stepping laterally.
- Jam the receiver with both hands while aiming for his pecks. He should not lunge. The defender should lock his elbows and deny the receiver an easy release, but

not lose his balance by being overly aggressive. He should not allow the receiver to get too close to him, by trying to maintain an arms-length distance.

- Punch the receiver's inside shoulder with his inside hand versus an inside release. He should slide parallel with the receiver and ride him down the line, denying the receiver an inside release.
- Open his hips slightly (without opening the gate) and get his inside hand on the receiver's inside shoulder versus an outside release.
- Trail the receiver at a distance that enables the defender to reach out and touch the receiver's back pocket. If the defender can't touch the receiver, there is too much separation between the two of them, and the cornerback must close the gap.
- Maintain inside leverage by keeping his body between the receiver and the ball.
- Concentrate on the receiver's hips and feet as he trails him.

Two-Man Techniques for Safeties

A defensive safety should:

- Line up 10 to 15 yards deep, on or near the hash marks.
- Be as deep as the deepest receiver in his half of the field, but not just cover air. He shouldn't go any deeper than necessary to cover his area.
- Use his peripheral vision to see the ball and the receivers at all times.
- Read the quarterback's eyes.
- Never break on the ball until it is thrown, but once it is thrown, go after it. He must expect that every pass (even those thrown away from him) will be tipped and that he will intercept it.
- Never go in front of a receiver to intercept a deep pass unless he's absolutely sure that he can get two hands on the ball.

STUNT #75

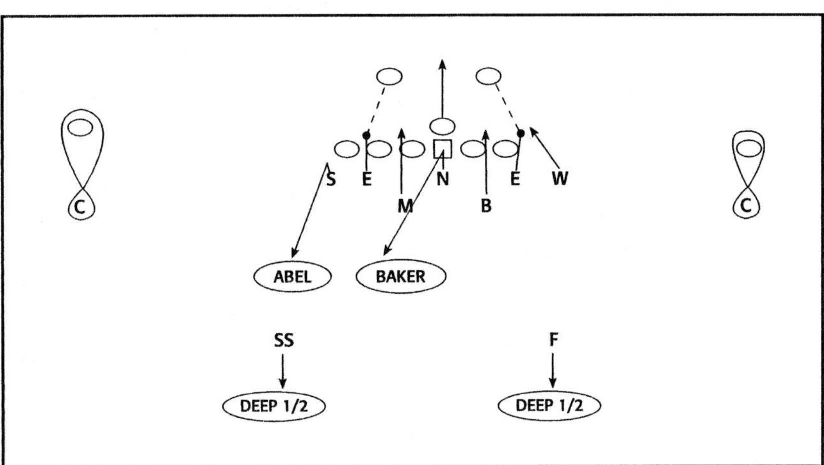

STUNT DESCRIPTION: This gumbo blitz incorporates illusion principles into its scheme.

SECONDARY COVERAGE: Cover 2 man. Stud and nose drop off into gumbo coverage, and the weak end spies.

STRONG SAFETY: Plays deep-half coverage.

STUD: Plays 9 technique versus run. Drops **Abel** gumbo versus pass.

STRONG END: Plays 5 technique versus run. Contains the quarterback versus pass.

MIKE: Blitzes through the outside shoulder of the offensive guard and secures the B gap.

NOSE: Plays 0 technique versus run. Drops **Baker** gumbo versus pass.

BUCK: Blitzes through the outside shoulder of the offensive guard and secures the B gap.

WEAK END: Plays 5 technique versus run. Spies the near back versus pass.

WHIP: Rushes from the edge. Contains the quarterback and weakside run. Chases strongside run.

FREE SAFETY: Plays deep-half coverage.

STRONG CORNER: Covers receiver #1 (jam technique).

WEAK CORNER: Covers receiver #1 (jam technique).

STUNT #76

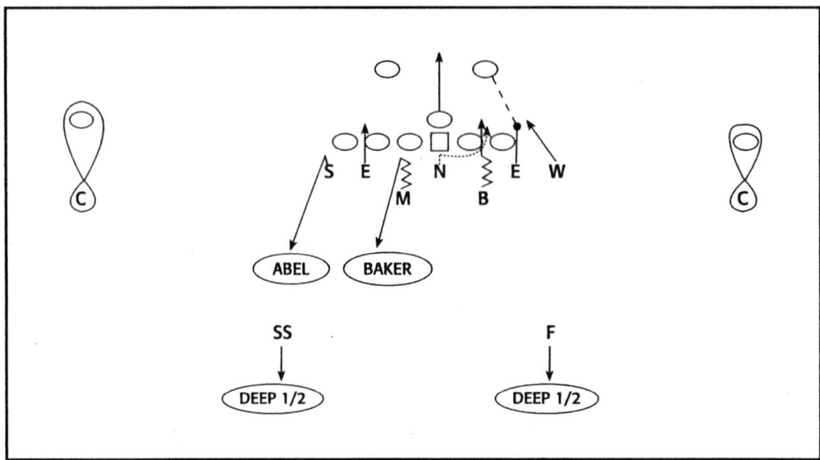

STUNT DESCRIPTION: This gumbo blitz incorporates weakside illusion principles and a delayed twin stunt into its scheme.

SECONDARY COVERAGE: Cover 2 man. Stud and Mike drop off into gumbo coverage, and the weak end spies.

STRONG SAFETY: Plays deep-half coverage.

STUD: Plays 9 technique versus run. Drops **Abel** gumbo versus pass.

STRONG END: Plays 5 technique versus run. Contains the quarterback versus pass.

MIKE: Shows blitz by creeping toward the line during cadence. Secures the B gap versus run and drops **Baker** gumbo versus pass.

NOSE: Plays 0 technique versus run. Delay rushes through the weakside B gap (twin stunt) versus pass.

BUCK: Creeps toward the line during cadence and blitzes through the outside shoulder of the offensive guard. Secures the B gap.

WEAK END: Plays 5 technique versus run. Spies the near back versus pass.

WHIP: Rushes from the edge. Contains the quarterback and weakside run. Chases strongside run.

FREE SAFETY: Plays deep-half coverage.

STRONG CORNER: Covers receiver #1 (jam technique).

WEAK CORNER: Covers receiver #1 (jam technique).

STUNT #77

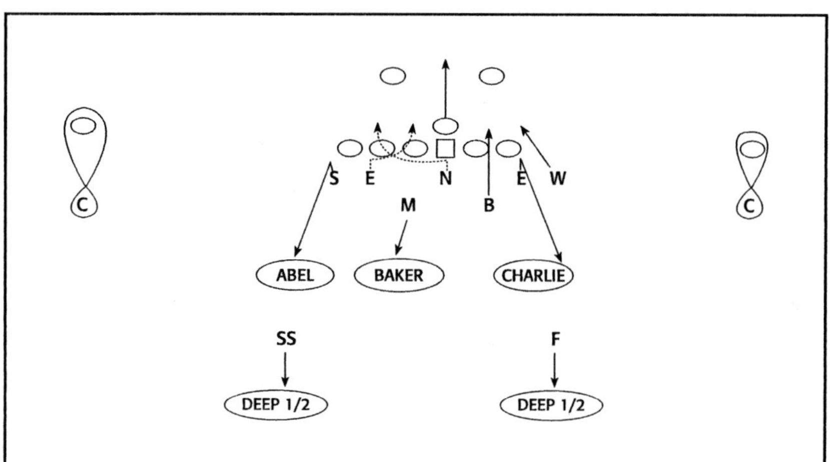

STUNT DESCRIPTION: This banjo blitz incorporates a delayed line twist into its scheme.

SECONDARY COVERAGE: Cover 2 man. Stud, Mike, and the weak end drop off into banjo coverage.

STRONG SAFETY: Plays deep-half coverage.

STUD: Plays 9 technique versus run. Drops **Abel** banjo versus pass.

STRONG END: Plays 5 technique versus run. Delay rushes through the B gap versus pass.

MIKE: Plays base technique versus run. Drops **Baker** banjo versus pass.

NOSE: Plays 0 technique versus run. Delay rushes through the strongside C gap, with quarterback containment responsibility, versus pass.

BUCK: Blitzes through the outside shoulder of the offensive guard and secures the B gap.

WEAK END: Plays 5 technique versus run. Drops **Charlie** banjo versus pass.

WHIP: Rushes from the edge. Contains the quarterback and weakside run. Chases strongside run.

FREE SAFETY: Plays deep-half coverage.

STRONG CORNER: Covers receiver #1 (jam technique).

WEAK CORNER: Covers receiver #1 (jam technique).

STUNT #78

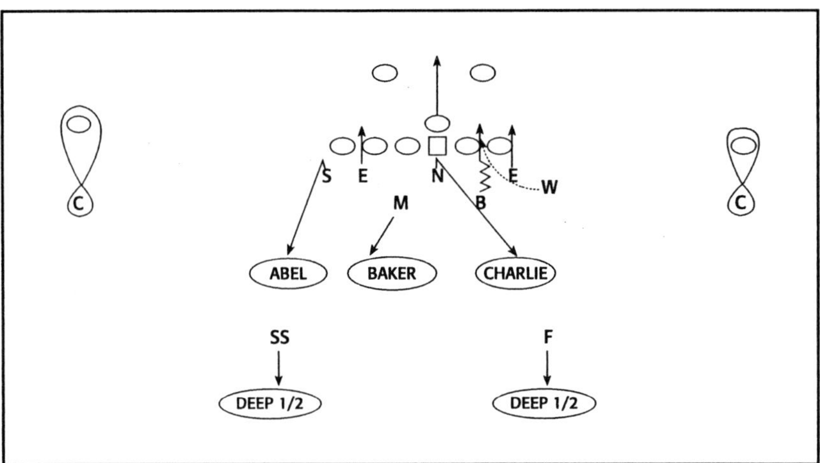

STUNT DESCRIPTION: This banjo blitz incorporates a weakside twin stunt into its scheme.

SECONDARY COVERAGE: Cover 2 man. Stud, Mike, and nose drop off into banjo coverage.

STRONG SAFETY: Plays deep-half coverage.

STUD: Plays 9 technique versus run. Drops **Abel** banjo versus pass.

STRONG END: Plays 5 technique versus run. Contains the quarterback versus pass.

MIKE: Plays base technique versus run. Drops **Baker** banjo versus pass.

NOSE: Plays 0 technique versus run. Drops **Charlie** banjo versus pass.

BUCK: Creeps toward the line during cadence and blitzes through the outside shoulder of the offensive guard.

WEAK END: Plays 5 technique versus run. Contains the quarterback versus pass.

WHIP: Plays 9 technique versus run. Delay rushes through the B gap (twin stunt) versus pass.

FREE SAFETY: Plays deep-half coverage.

STRONG CORNER: Covers receiver #1 (jam technique).

WEAK CORNER: Covers receiver #1 (jam technique).

STUNT #79

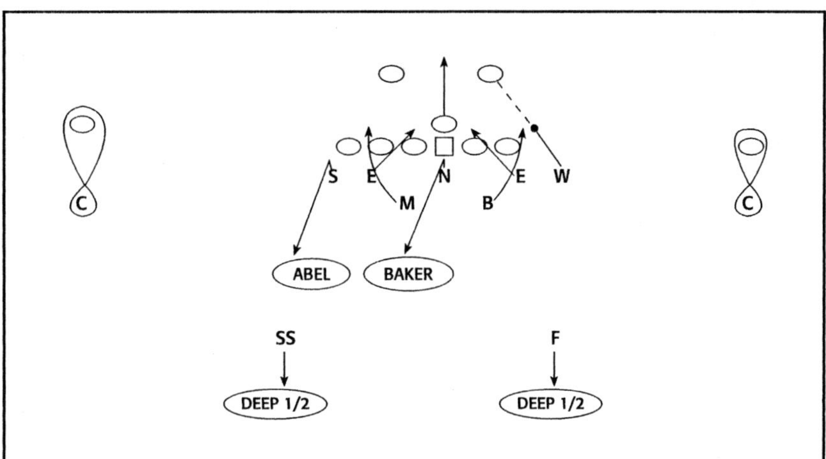

STUNT DESCRIPTION: This gumbo blitz incorporates illusion principles into its scheme.

SECONDARY COVERAGE: Cover 2 man. Stud and nose drop off into gumbo coverage, and Whip spies the near back.

STRONG SAFETY: Plays deep-half coverage.

STUD: Plays 9 technique versus run. Drops **Abel** gumbo versus pass.

STRONG END: Slants across the face of the offensive tackle into the B gap.

MIKE: Blitzes through the outside shoulder of the offensive tackle, secures the C gap, and contains the quarterback.

NOSE: Plays 0 technique versus run. Drops **Baker** gumbo versus pass.

BUCK: Blitzes through the outside shoulder of the offensive tackle, secures the C gap, and contains the quarterback.

WEAK END: Slants across the face of the offensive tackle into the B gap.

WHIP: Pretends to rush from the edge. Secures the D gap versus run and spies the near back versus pass.

FREE SAFETY: Plays deep-half coverage.

STRONG CORNER: Covers receiver #1 (jam technique).

WEAK CORNER: Covers receiver #1 (jam technique).

STUNT #80

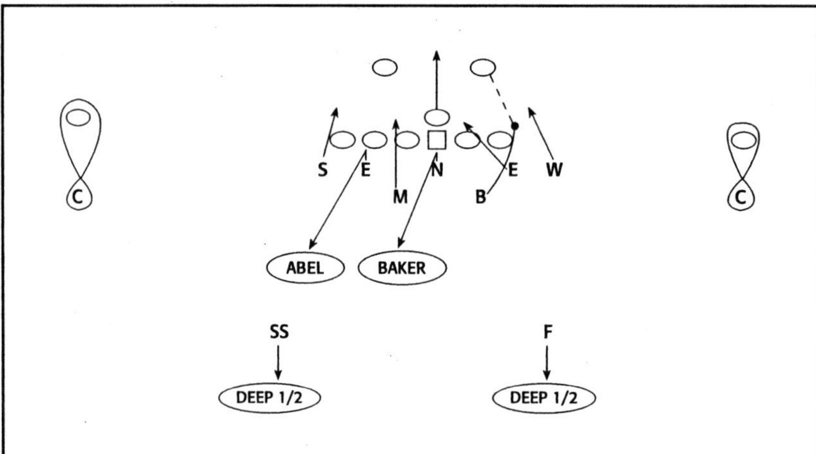

STUNT DESCRIPTION: This gumbo blitz incorporates illusion principles into its scheme.

SECONDARY COVERAGE: Cover 2 man. Stud and nose drop off into gumbo coverage, and Buck spies the near back.

STRONG SAFETY: Plays deep-half coverage.

STUD: Plays 9 technique versus run. Contains the quarterback versus pass.

STRONG END: Plays 5 technique versus run. Drops **Abel** gumbo versus pass.

MIKE: Blitzes through the outside shoulder of the offensive guard and secures the B gap.

NOSE: Plays 0 technique versus run. Drops **Baker** gumbo versus pass.

BUCK: Fakes a blitz into the C gap. Secures the C gap versus run and spies the near back versus pass.

WEAK END: Slants across the face of the offensive tackle into the B gap.

WHIP: Rushes from the edge. Contains the quarterback and weakside run. Chases strongside run.

FREE SAFETY: Plays deep-half coverage.

STRONG CORNER: Covers receiver #1 (jam technique).

WEAK CORNER: Covers receiver #1 (jam technique).

STUNT #81

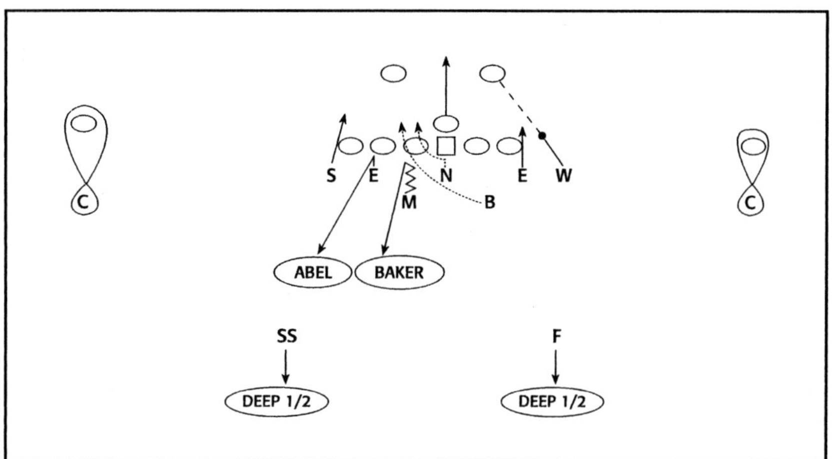

STUNT DESCRIPTION: This gumbo blitz incorporates delayed rushes into its scheme.

SECONDARY COVERAGE: Cover 2 man. Stud and Mike drop off into gumbo coverage, and Whip spies the near back.

STRONG SAFETY: Plays deep-half coverage.

STUD: Plays 9 technique versus run. Contains the quarterback versus pass.

STRONG END: Plays 5 technique versus run. Drops **Abel** gumbo versus pass.

MIKE: Threatens to blitz through the outside shoulder of the offensive guard by creeping toward the line during cadence. Secures the B gap versus run and drops **Baker** gumbo versus pass.

NOSE: Plays 0 technique versus run. Delay rushes through the inside shoulder of the strongside guard versus pass.

BUCK: Plays base technique versus run. Delay blitzes through the outside shoulder of the strongside guard versus pass.

WEAK END: Plays 5 technique versus run. Contains the quarterback versus pass.

WHIP: Plays 9 technique versus run. Spies the near back versus pass.

FREE SAFETY: Plays deep-half coverage.

STRONG CORNER: Covers receiver #1 (jam technique).

WEAK CORNER: Covers receiver #1 (jam technique).

CHAPTER 6

ZONE COVERAGE STUNTS

Before presenting the zone coverage stunts, I will explain some of the assignments, techniques, and pattern reads that defenders should utilize when employing the following zone drops: Curl-out drop, Hook-curl drop, Deep-middle-third drop, Deep-outside-third drop, Deep-half drop, or Cornerback cover 2 zone technique.

CURL-OUT DROP

General defensive information

Versus a pro formation, the defender opens up and aims for a spot 10 yards deep, and in front of where receiver #1 originally lines up. The defender must keep his head on a swivel and be aware of how many steps the quarterback takes. He adjusts his drop to receiver #1's route. The defender listens for an *"out-out"* call by the defender dropping hook-curl, and an *"in-in"* call by the corners. He plays the deepest receiver in his zone and rallies up to the short routes after the ball has been thrown.

Versus Quick 3-Step Patterns (Hitches, Outs, Slants, etc.)

The defender tries to get into the throwing lane. He will probably arrive too late to intercept or tip these patterns, but he can arrive in time to punish the receiver and strip the ball. He should remember that wide receivers are usually not the most courageous players on the field, and he can discourage them from entering his zone again.

Versus 5- and 7-Step, Out and Comeback Routes

The defender plays these routes from an inside-out position. He tries to get into the throwing lane and force the quarterback to throw the ball over his hands. He should always be looking to strip the ball and punish the receiver.

Versus the Curl

The defender should know that this pattern is usually accompanied by an out pattern by receiver #2. He positions himself three yards inside of, and underneath, the curl. He tries to maintain an inside-out-and-under position on both the receiver and the ball. If receiver #2's out route crosses his face, he gradually widens out, but doesn't jump the out pattern too quickly. He first makes sure that he has help from the defender dropping hook-curl. If he jumps out too quickly, he will be giving up a 12- to 18-yard pattern in order to stop a 5-yard pattern.

Versus the Post, Post-Corner, and Streak Routes

If receiver #1 runs a vertical route (streak, fade, post-corner, etc.), the defender checks receiver #2 and listens for an *"out-out"* call. If no *"out-out"* call occurs, then he runs with the vertical route and, if possible, collisions it. He should look over his inside shoulder to find the ball. If he gets a *"post"* call from the cornerback, he tries to get under the route if receiver #2 does not threaten him.

HOOK-CURL DROP

General defensive information

The defender opens outside and drops 12- to 15-yards deep. The field position and the formation determine the width of his drop. Versus a pro formation, he reads receiver #2 and then #1, and listens for a *"cross"* call from the defender dropping hook-curl. Both defenders dropping hook-curl play the deepest receivers in their zones and rally up to the short receiver patterns.

Versus Vertical Release by Receiver #2

The defender gets to a position one yard inside and underneath the receiver. If the receiver hooks inside, the defender walls him off by using a hand shove. The defender cannot let the receiver get into the middle hook zone. If the receiver hooks outside, the defender breaks for an inside-out position and tries to strip the ball. If the receiver streaks, the defender should collision him and sink. If he gets an *"in-in"* call from the other defender who's dropping hook-curl, he should hang in the hook and play the deepest receiver. If there is no *"in-in"* call, he should check curl.

Versus Flare or Flat Release by Receiver #2

The defender should sprint to the curl, locate the widest receiver, and give an *"out-out"* call. He should get to a position three yards inside and underneath the widest receiver if he is running a curl. The defender should maintain an inside-out position, and not overrun the ball. If the widest receiver runs a post, the defender should pivot inside and get additional depth.

Versus a Crossing Route by Receiver #2

If receiver #2 crosses deeper than five yards, the defender should try to ward him off and jam him as far as the center of the field. As the defender releases him, he calls *"cross."* If the receiver crosses shallow, the defender squares up and continues to drop. He calls *"cross"* and looks for a complementary crossing route by the receiver from the opposite side, or a curl or post by receiver #1.

Versus a Seam by Receiver #2

Defenders will usually see this when they play sprint-out teams. The defensive back must get additional width and make his drop to the receiver. He tries to get into the throwing lane, sprints for the receiver's outside hip and comes underneath.

Versus Play-Action

If the defensive back is aligned on the playside, he opens outside and reads the widest receiver. If he is on the backside, he must recognize that the ball is still in the pocket and the possibility of a throwback exists. He opens and gets under the curl or post, and reacts up to crossing patterns from the opposite side.

Versus Sprint, Waggle, or Bootleg

If the defender is aligned on the playside, he opens outside and reads receiver #2. If he is on the backside, he must recognize that the ball is out of the pocket, and the possibility of a throwback exists. He drops to deep-middle hook, and slides with the quarterback. He has to locate and cover crossing patterns.

DEEP-MIDDLE-THIRD DROP

General defensive information

The defender keys the ball to the receivers. He shuffles two steps in the direction of the ball. His drop angle must put him midway between the cornerbacks versus a dropback pass. Versus a pro formation, he keys the tight end's release. If the release is vertical, he must be prepared to go deep. If receiver #2's release is short or away from the defender, he looks for a post from the two widest receivers. He must not react to a short or intermediate route as long as there is a deep threat.

DEEP-OUTSIDE-THIRD DROP

General defensive information

The defender keys the ball to the receiver. During a dropback pass, he should see receivers #1 and #2 on his side. If both receivers run short or intermediate routes, he continues to control the speed of his backpedal so he is in a good position to break on the ball. If receiver #1 runs a short or intermediate route (out, curl, etc.), the defender reads receiver #2, since he can threaten deep third. If both receivers go away from him, the defender squeezes the field, keeping his outside leverage on the deepest receiver.

DEEP-HALF DROP

General defensive information

The defender stays as deep as the deepest receiver. He reads both receiver #1 and #2 on his side, and works toward the receiver who goes deepest. If both receivers go deep, he moves outside of #2 so that he is able to break to #1.

CORNERBACK'S COVER 2 ZONE TECHNIQUE

General defensive information

The defender jams receiver #1 and stays on his outside shoulder, funneling him inside, and not allowing him an outside release. At the same time, the defender watches the release of receiver #2. If receiver #2 releases short into the flat, the defender gains depth and width but doesn't react to him until he crosses the defender's face. If receiver #2 runs a wheel route, the defender collisions and runs with him. If receiver #2 runs a vertical or crossing route, the defender stays with #1 unless threatened by #3. If receiver #3 releases into the flats, the defender must be in a position to rally up.

STUNT #82

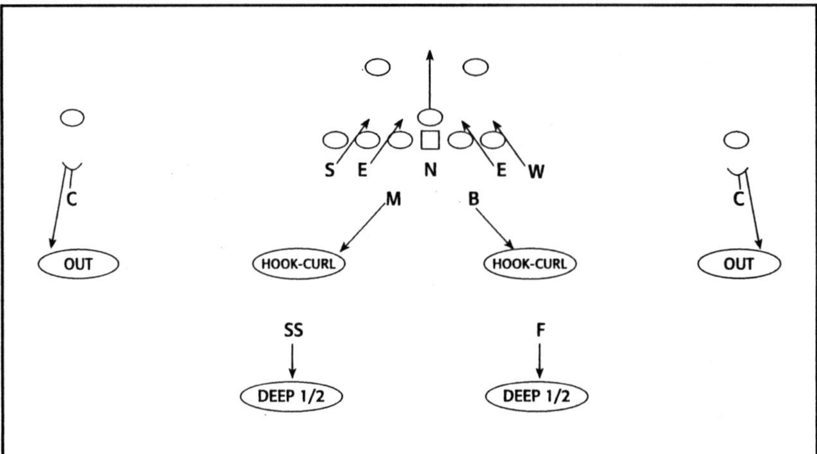

STUNT DESCRIPTION: This stunt gives the defense a five-man pass rush.

SECONDARY COVERAGE: This is a 4-under/2-deep zone. Mike and Buck drop off into the under coverage.

STRONG SAFETY: Plays deep-half coverage.

STUD: Slants across the face of the tight end into the C gap. Controls the C gap versus run and contains the quarterback versus pass.

STRONG END: Slants into the B gap.

MIKE: Scrapes outside and contains versus strongside run. Pursues weakside run from an inside-out position. Drops hook-curl versus pass.

NOSE: Plays 0 technique.

BUCK: Scrapes outside and contains versus weakside run. Pursues strongside run from an inside-out position. Drops hook-curl versus pass.

WEAK END: Slants into the B gap.

WHIP: Rushes through the outside shoulder of the offensive tackle. Secures the C gap and contains the quarterback.

FREE SAFETY: Plays deep-half coverage.

STRONG CORNER: Funnels receiver #1 into the curl and sinks back to the out if threatened by receiver #2.

WEAK CORNER: Funnels receiver #1 into the curl and sinks back to the out if threatened by receiver #2.

STUNT #83

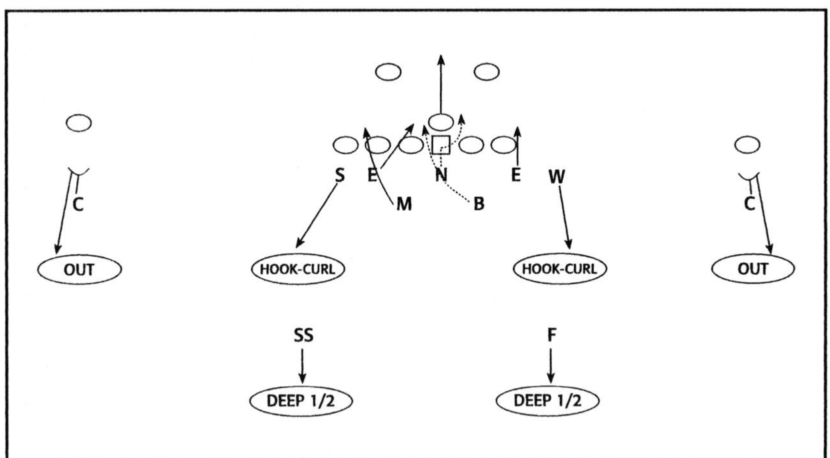

STUNT DESCRIPTION: This stunt gives the defense a five-man pass rush and features a delayed pass rush by Buck.

SECONDARY COVERAGE: This is a 4-under/2-deep zone. Stud and Whip drop off into the under coverage.

STRONG SAFETY: Plays deep-half coverage.

STUD: Plays 9 technique versus run. Drops hook-curl versus pass.

STRONG END: Slants into the B gap.

MIKE: Blitzes through the outside shoulder of the offensive tackle, secures the C gap, and contains the quarterback.

NOSE: Plays 0 technique versus run. Engages the center's block long enough so that the center doesn't pick up Buck's blitz. He then directs his rush to the weakside A gap versus pass.

BUCK: Plays base technique versus run. Delay blitzes through the strongside A gap versus pass.

WEAK END: Plays 5 technique versus run. Contains the quarterback versus pass.

WHIP: Plays 9 technique versus run. Drops hook-curl versus pass.

FREE SAFETY: Plays deep-half coverage.

STRONG CORNER: Funnels receiver #1 into the curl and sinks back to the out if threatened by receiver #2.

WEAK CORNER: Funnels receiver #1 into the curl and sinks back to the out if threatened by receiver #2.

STUNT #84

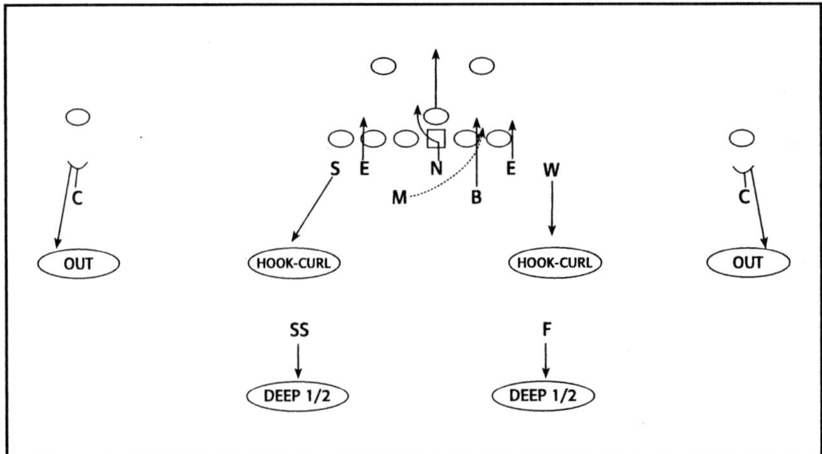

STUNT DESCRIPTION: This stunt gives the defense a five-man pass rush and features a delayed pass rush by Mike.

SECONDARY COVERAGE: This is a 4-under/2-deep zone. Stud and Whip drop off into the under coverage.

STRONG SAFETY: Plays deep-half coverage.

STUD: Plays 9 technique versus run. Drops hook-curl versus pass.

STRONG END: Plays 5 technique versus run. Contains the quarterback versus pass.

MIKE: Plays base technique versus run. Delay blitzes through the weakside B gap versus pass.

NOSE: Plays 0 technique versus run. Engages the center's block and then directs his rush to the strongside A gap versus pass.

BUCK: Blitzes through the outside shoulder of the offensive guard and secures the B gap.

WEAK END: Plays 5 technique versus run. Contains the quarterback versus pass.

WHIP: Plays 9 technique versus run. Drops hook-curl versus pass.

FREE SAFETY: Plays deep-half coverage.

STRONG CORNER: Funnels receiver #1 into the curl and sinks back to the out if threatened by receiver #2.

WEAK CORNER: Funnels receiver #1 into the curl and sinks back to the out if threatened by receiver #2.

STUNT #85

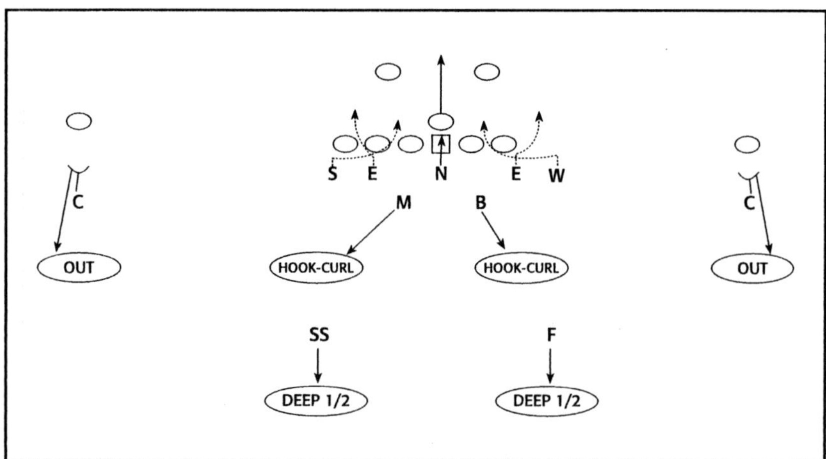

STUNT DESCRIPTION: This stunt gives the defense a five-man pass rush that features a delayed twist by Stud and Whip.

SECONDARY COVERAGE: This is a 4-under/2-deep zone. Mike and Buck drop off into the under coverage.

STRONG SAFETY: Plays deep-half coverage.

STUD: Plays 9 technique versus run. Loops into the B gap versus pass.

STRONG END: Plays 5 technique versus run. Quickly penetrates the C gap and contains the quarterback versus pass.

MIKE: Plays base technique versus run. Drops hook-curl versus pass.

NOSE: Plays 0 technique.

BUCK: Plays base technique versus run. Drops hook-curl versus pass.

WEAK END: Plays 5 technique versus run. Quickly penetrates the C gap and contains the quarterback versus pass.

WHIP: Plays 9 technique versus run. Loops into the B gap versus pass.

FREE SAFETY: Plays deep-half coverage.

STRONG CORNER: Funnels receiver #1 into the curl and sinks back to the out if threatened by receiver #2.

WEAK CORNER: Funnels receiver #1 into the curl and sinks back to the out if threatened by receiver #2.

STUNT #86

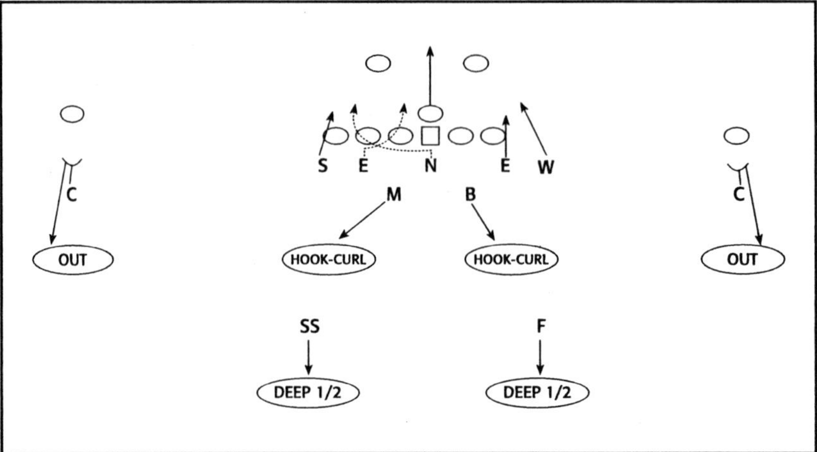

STUNT DESCRIPTION: This stunt gives the defense a five-man pass rush that features a delayed line twist.

SECONDARY COVERAGE: This is a 4-under/2-deep zone. Mike and Buck drop off into the under coverage.

STRONG SAFETY: Plays deep-half coverage.

STUD: Plays 9 technique versus run. Contains the quarterback versus pass.

STRONG END: Plays 5 technique versus run. Slants inside and quickly penetrates the B gap versus pass.

MIKE: Plays base technique versus run. Drops hook-curl versus pass.

NOSE: Plays 0 technique versus run. Loops through the outside shoulder of the strongside tackle and contains the quarterback versus pass.

BUCK: Plays base technique versus run. Drops hook-curl versus pass.

WEAK END: Plays 5 technique versus run. Contains the quarterback versus pass.

WHIP: Rushes from the edge. Contains the quarterback and weakside run. Chases strongside run.

FREE SAFETY: Plays deep-half coverage.

STRONG CORNER: Funnels receiver #1 into the curl and sinks back to the out if threatened by receiver #2.

WEAK CORNER: Funnels receiver #1 into the curl and sinks back to the out if threatened by receiver #2.

STUNT #87

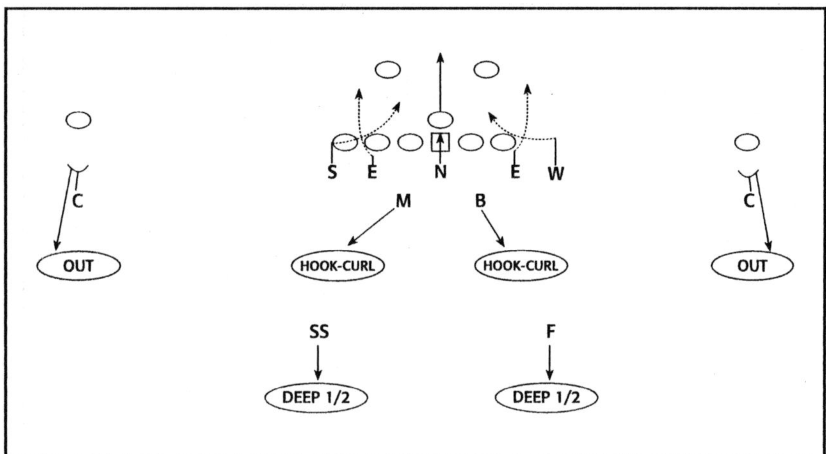

STUNT DESCRIPTION: This stunt gives the defense a five-man pass rush that features a delayed twist by Stud and Whip.

SECONDARY COVERAGE: This is a 4-under/2-deep zone. Mike and Buck drop off into the under coverage.

STRONG SAFETY: Plays deep-half coverage.

STUD: Plays 9 technique versus run. Versus pass, he appears to be on a contain rush, but as he feels the defensive end gaining penetration and depth, he loops inside.

STRONG END: Plays 5 technique versus run. Quickly penetrates the C gap and contains the quarterback versus pass. His quick penetration is imperative!

MIKE: Plays base technique versus run. Drops hook-curl versus pass.

NOSE: Plays 0 technique.

BUCK: Plays base technique versus run. Drops hook-curl versus pass.

WEAK END: Plays 5 technique versus run. Quickly penetrates the C gap and contains the quarterback versus pass. His quick penetration is imperative!

WHIP: Plays 9 technique versus run. Versus pass, he appears to be on a contain rush, but as he feels the defensive end gaining penetration and depth, he loops inside.

FREE SAFETY: Plays deep-half coverage.

STRONG CORNER: Funnels receiver #1 into the curl and sinks back to the out if threatened by receiver #2.

WEAK CORNER: Funnels receiver #1 into the curl and sinks back to the out if threatened by receiver #2.

STUNT #88

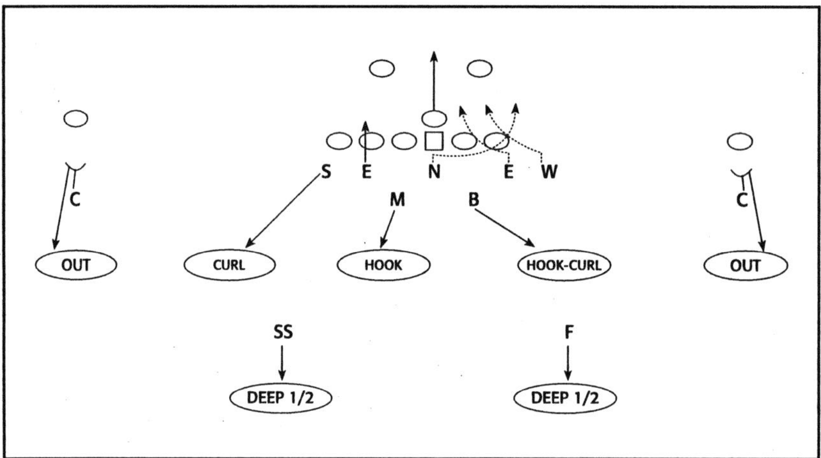

STUNT DESCRIPTION: This stunt gives the defense a five-man pass rush that features a delayed twist by the nose, Whip, and the weak end. The weakness of the stunt is that the pass rush is unbalanced. There are a number of unbalanced pass rushes included in this book because an unbalanced pass rush can be an effective tactic when a team has a tendency to release a specific halfback and use the other halfback as a pass blocker.

SECONDARY COVERAGE: This is a 5-under/2-deep zone. Stud, Mike, and Buck drop off into the under coverage.

STRONG SAFETY: Plays deep-half coverage.

STUD: Plays 9 technique versus run. Drops curl versus pass.

STRONG END: Plays 5 technique versus run. Contains the quarterback versus pass.

MIKE: Plays base technique versus run. Drops hook versus pass.

NOSE: Plays 0 technique versus run. Loops across the face of the weakside tackle and contains the quarterback versus pass.

BUCK: Plays base technique versus run. Drops hook-curl versus pass

WEAK END: Plays 5 technique versus run. Slants across the face of the offensive tackle and quickly penetrates the B gap versus pass.

WHIP: Plays 9 technique versus run. Rushes through the C gap versus pass.

FREE SAFETY: Plays deep-half coverage.

STRONG CORNER: Funnels receiver #1 into the curl and sinks back to the out if threatened by receiver #2.

WEAK CORNER: Funnels receiver #1 into the curl and sinks back to the out if threatened by receiver #2.

STUNT #89

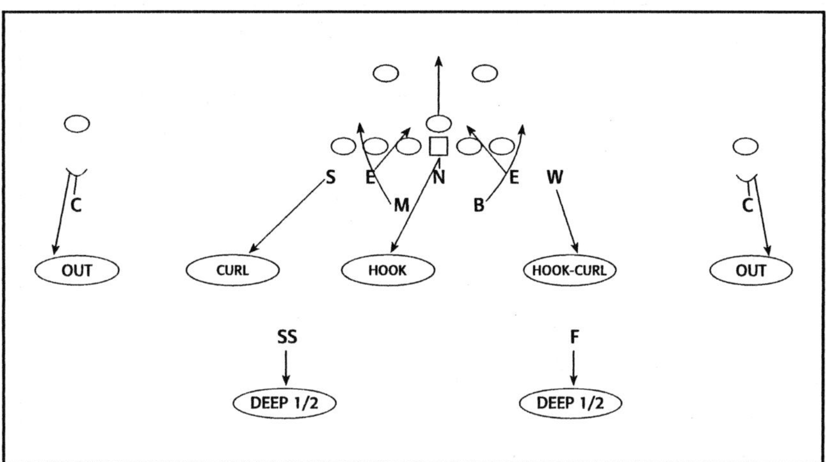

STUNT DESCRIPTION: This stunt incorporates zone blitz principles into its scheme.

SECONDARY COVERAGE: This is a 5-under/2-deep zone. Stud, nose, and Whip drop off into the under coverage.

STRONG SAFETY: Plays deep-half coverage.

STUD: Plays 9 technique versus run. Drops curl versus pass.

STRONG END: Slants across the offensive tackle's face into the B gap.

MIKE: Blitzes through the outside shoulder of the offensive tackle. Secures the C gap and contains the quarterback.

NOSE: Plays 0 technique versus run. Drops hook versus pass.

BUCK: Blitzes through the outside shoulder of the offensive tackle. Secures the C gap and contains the quarterback.

WEAK END: Slants across the offensive tackle's face into the B gap.

WHIP: Plays 9 technique versus run. Drops hook-curl versus pass.

FREE SAFETY: Plays deep-half coverage.

STRONG CORNER: Funnels receiver #1 into the curl and sinks back to the out if threatened by receiver #2.

WEAK CORNER: Funnels receiver #1 into the curl and sinks back to the out if threatened by receiver #2.

STUNT #90

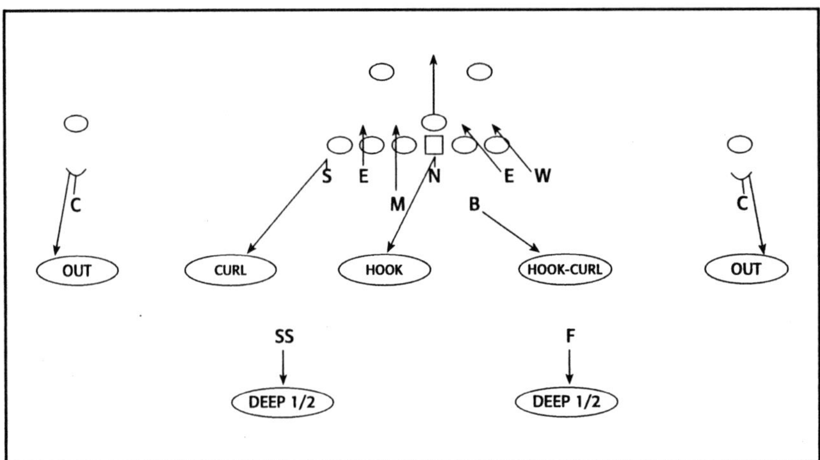

STUNT DESCRIPTION: This stunt incorporates zone blitz principles into its scheme.

SECONDARY COVERAGE: This is a 5-under/2-deep zone. Stud, nose, and Buck drop off into the under coverage.

STRONG SAFETY: Plays deep-half coverage.

STUD: Plays 9 technique versus run. Drops curl versus pass.

STRONG END: Plays 5 technique versus run. Contains the quarterback versus pass.

MIKE: Blitzes through the outside shoulder of the offensive guard and secures the B gap.

NOSE: Plays 0 technique versus run. Drops hook versus pass.

BUCK: Scrapes outside and contains versus weakside run. Pursues strongside run from an inside-out position. Drops hook-curl versus pass.

WEAK END: Slants across the offensive tackle's face into the B gap.

WHIP: Rushes through the outside shoulder of the offensive tackle. Secures the C gap and contains the quarterback.

FREE SAFETY: Plays deep-half coverage.

STRONG CORNER: Funnels receiver #1 into the curl and sinks back to the out if threatened by receiver #2.

WEAK CORNER: Funnels receiver #1 into the curl and sinks back to the out if threatened by receiver #2.

STUNT #91

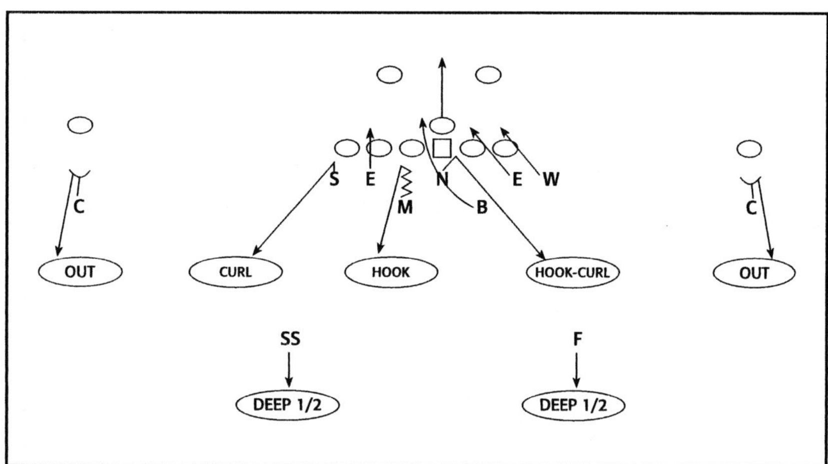

STUNT DESCRIPTION: This stunt incorporates zone blitz principles into its scheme. It is excellent versus pass and strongside run but not advisable versus weakside run.

SECONDARY COVERAGE: This is a 5-under/2-deep zone. Stud, nose, and Mike drop off into the under coverage.

STRONG SAFETY: Plays deep-half coverage.

STUD: Plays 9 technique versus run. Drops curl versus pass.

STRONG END: Plays 5 technique versus run. Contains the quarterback versus pass.

MIKE: Creeps slowly toward the line as though he's going to blitz. Secures the B gap versus run and drops hook versus pass.

NOSE: Slants to and controls the weakside A gap versus run. Drops hook-curl (weak) versus pass.

BUCK: Blitzes through the strongside A gap.

WEAK END: Slants across the offensive tackle's face into the B gap.

WHIP: Rushes through the outside shoulder of the offensive tackle. Secures the C gap and contains the quarterback.

FREE SAFETY: Plays deep-half coverage.

STRONG CORNER: Funnels receiver #1 into the curl and sinks back to the out if threatened by receiver #2.

WEAK CORNER: Funnels receiver #1 into the curl and sinks back to the out if threatened by receiver #2.

STUNT #92

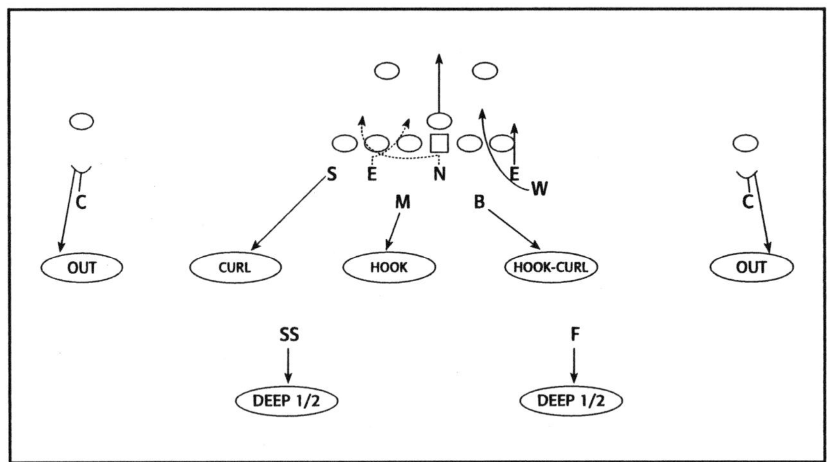

STUNT DESCRIPTION: This stunt incorporates a delayed line twist into its scheme.

SECONDARY COVERAGE: This is a 5-under/2-deep zone. Stud, Mike, and Buck drop off into the under coverage.

STRONG SAFETY: Plays deep-half coverage.

STUD: Plays 9 technique versus run. Drops curl versus pass.

STRONG END: Plays 5 technique versus run. Slants inside and quickly penetrates the B gap versus pass.

MIKE: Plays base technique versus run. Drops hook versus pass.

NOSE: Plays 0 technique versus run. Loops through the outside shoulder of the strongside tackle and contains the quarterback versus pass.

BUCK: Scrapes outside and contains versus weakside run. Pursues strongside run from an inside-out position. Drops hook-curl versus pass.

WEAK END: Plays 5 technique versus run. Contains the quarterback versus pass.

WHIP: Cheats back slightly and blitzes through the B gap.

FREE SAFETY: Plays deep-half coverage.

STRONG CORNER: Funnels receiver #1 into the curl and sinks back to the out if threatened by receiver #2.

WEAK CORNER: Funnels receiver #1 into the curl and sinks back to the out if threatened by receiver #2.

STUNT #93

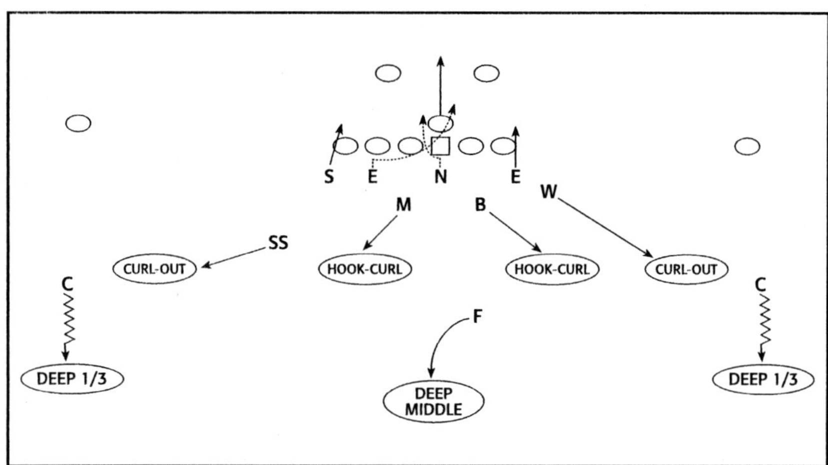

STUNT DESCRIPTION: This stunt incorporates a delayed line twist into its scheme.

SECONDARY COVERAGE: This is a 4-under/3-deep zone. The strong safety, Mike, Buck, and Whip drop off into the under coverage.

STRONG SAFETY: Contains strongside run. Checks throwback versus weakside run. Drops curl-out versus dropback pass.

STUD: Plays 9 technique versus run. Contains the quarterback versus pass.

STRONG END: Plays 5 technique versus run. Slants into the strongside A gap versus pass. If blocked, he gradually works his way to the weakside and balances the pass rush.

MIKE: Plays base technique versus run. Drops hook-curl versus pass.

NOSE: Plays 0 technique versus run. Quickly penetrates the strongside A gap versus pass.

BUCK: Plays base technique versus run. Drops hook-curl versus pass.

WEAK END: Plays 5 technique versus run. Contains the quarterback versus pass.

WHIP: Plays 9 technique versus run. Drops curl-out versus pass.

FREE SAFETY: Plays deep-middle-third coverage.

STRONG CORNER: Plays deep-outside-third coverage.

WEAK CORNER: Plays deep-outside-third coverage.

STUNT #94

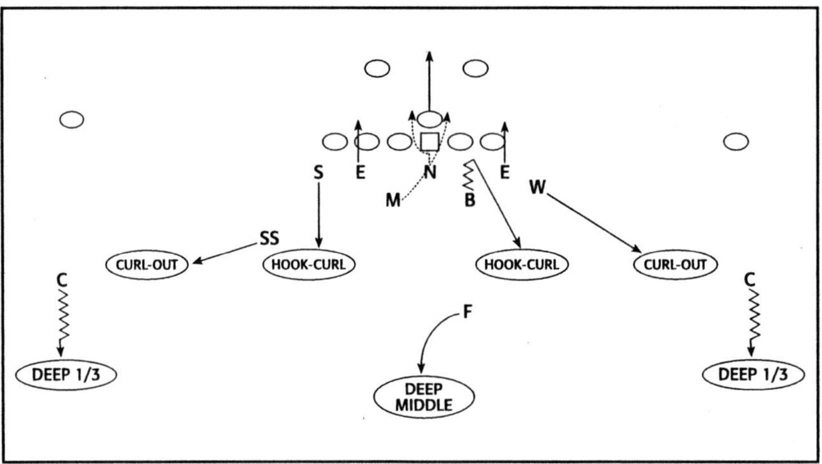

STUNT DESCRIPTION: This stunt incorporates a delayed linebacker blitz into its scheme.

SECONDARY COVERAGE: This is a 4-under/3-deep zone. The strong safety, Stud, Buck, and Whip drop off into the under coverage.

STRONG SAFETY: Contains strongside run. Checks throwback versus weakside run. Drops curl-out versus dropback pass.

STUD: Plays 9 technique versus run. Drops hook-curl versus pass.

STRONG END: Plays 5 technique versus run. Contains the quarterback versus pass.

MIKE: Plays base technique versus run. Delay blitzes through the outside shoulder of the center versus pass.

NOSE: Plays 0 technique versus run. Quickly penetrates the strongside A gap versus pass.

BUCK: Creeps toward the line as though he's going to blitz. Secures the B gap versus run and drops hook-curl versus pass.

WEAK END: Plays 5 technique versus run. Contains the quarterback versus pass.

WHIP: Plays 9 technique versus run. Drops curl-out versus pass.

FREE SAFETY: Plays deep-middle-third coverage.

STRONG CORNER: Plays deep-outside-third coverage.

WEAK CORNER: Plays deep-outside-third coverage.

STUNT #95

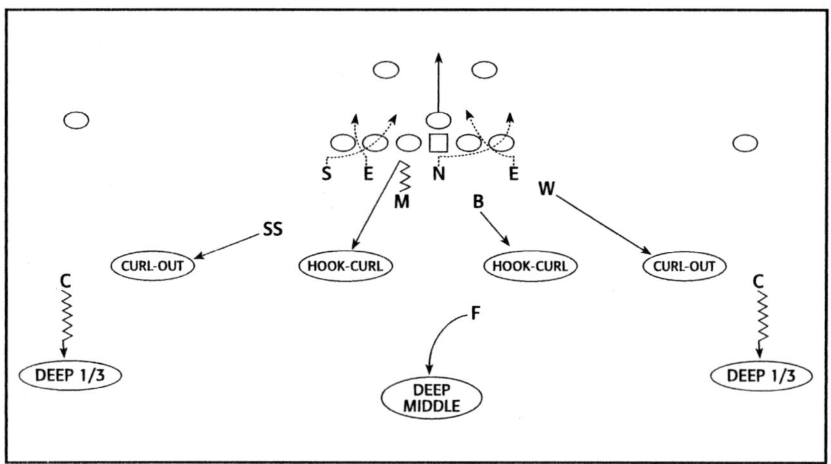

STUNT DESCRIPTION: This stunt incorporates two delayed twists into its scheme.

SECONDARY COVERAGE: This is a 4-under/3-deep zone. The strong safety, Mike, Buck, and Whip drop off into the under coverage.

STRONG SAFETY: Contains strongside run. Checks throwback versus weakside run. Drops curl-out versus dropback pass.

STUD: Plays 9 technique versus run. Delay blitzes through the inside shoulder of the offensive tackle versus pass.

STRONG END: Plays 5 technique versus run. Quickly penetrates the C gap and contains the quarterback versus pass.

MIKE: Creeps toward the line as though he's going to blitz. Secures the B gap versus run and drops hook-curl versus pass.

NOSE: Plays 0 technique versus run. Quickly loops through the weakside B gap and works for outside containment versus pass.

BUCK: Plays base technique versus run. Drops hook-curl versus pass.

WEAK END: Plays 5 technique versus run. Quickly slants inside and penetrates the B gap versus pass.

WHIP: Plays 9 technique versus run. Drops curl-out versus pass.

FREE SAFETY: Plays deep-middle-third coverage.

STRONG CORNER: Plays deep-outside-third coverage.

WEAK CORNER: Plays deep-outside-third coverage.

STUNT #96

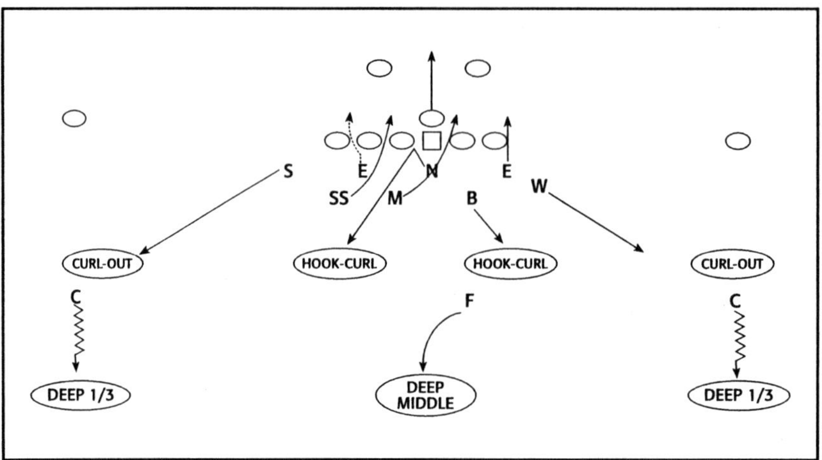

STUNT DESCRIPTION: This stunt features a strong-safety blitz and incorporates zone blitz principles into its scheme.

SECONDARY COVERAGE: This is a 4-under/3-deep zone. Stud, nose, Buck, and Whip drop off into the under coverage.

STRONG SAFETY: Lines up inside shade on the tight end, 4 to 5 yards deep. Blitzes through the B gap at the snap.

STUD: Plays loose 8 technique versus run. Drops curl-out versus pass.

STRONG END: Plays 5 technique versus run. Quickly penetrates the C gap and contains the quarterback versus pass.

MIKE: Blitzes through the weakside A gap at the snap.

NOSE: Slants to and secures the strongside A gap versus run. Drops strongside hook-curl versus pass.

BUCK: Plays base technique versus run. Drops hook-curl versus pass.

WEAK END: Plays 5 technique versus run. Contains the quarterback versus pass.

WHIP: Plays 9 technique versus run. Drops curl-out versus pass.

FREE SAFETY: Plays deep-middle-third coverage.

STRONG CORNER: Plays deep-outside-third coverage.

WEAK CORNER: Plays deep-outside-third coverage.

STUNT #97

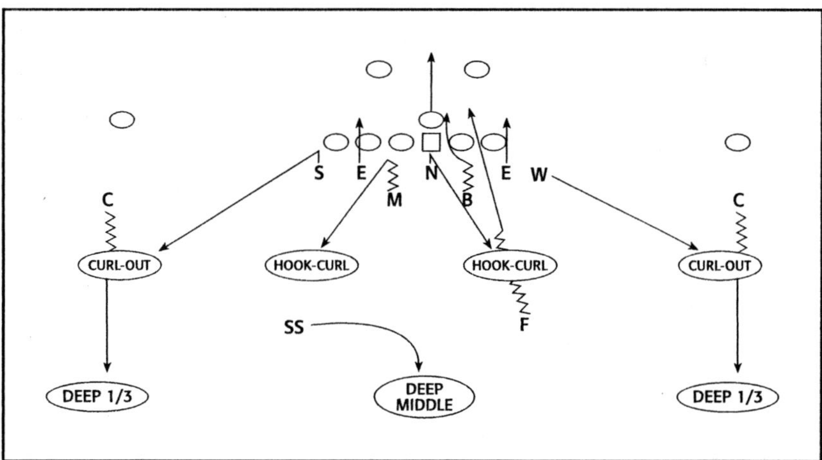

STUNT DESCRIPTION: This stunt features a free-safety blitz and incorporates zone blitz principles into its scheme.

SECONDARY COVERAGE: This is a 4-under/3-deep zone. Stud, Mike, nose, and Whip drop off into the under coverage.

STRONG SAFETY: Lines up in a cover 2 disguise and drops into the deep middle third at the snap.

STUD: Plays 9 technique versus run. Drops curl-out versus pass.

STRONG END: Plays 5 technique versus run. Contains the quarterback versus pass.

MIKE: Creeps toward the line as though he's going to blitz. Secures the B gap versus run and drops hook-curl versus pass.

NOSE: Plays 0 technique versus run. Drops weakside hook-curl versus pass.

BUCK: Creeps toward the line during cadence and gives the offensive guard the impression that he's going to blitz through the guard's outside shoulder. Blitzes through the A gap as the ball is snapped.

WEAK END: Plays 5 technique versus run. Contains the quarterback versus pass.

WHIP: Plays 9 technique versus run. Drops curl-out versus pass.

FREE SAFETY: Lines up in a cover 2 disguise but moves toward the line during cadence and blitzes through the weakside B gap.

STRONG CORNER: Lines up in a cover 2 disguise but moves to a position during cadence that enables him to cover the deep outside third.

WEAK CORNER: Lines up in a cover 2 disguise but moves to a position during cadence that enables him to cover the deep outside third.

STUNT #98

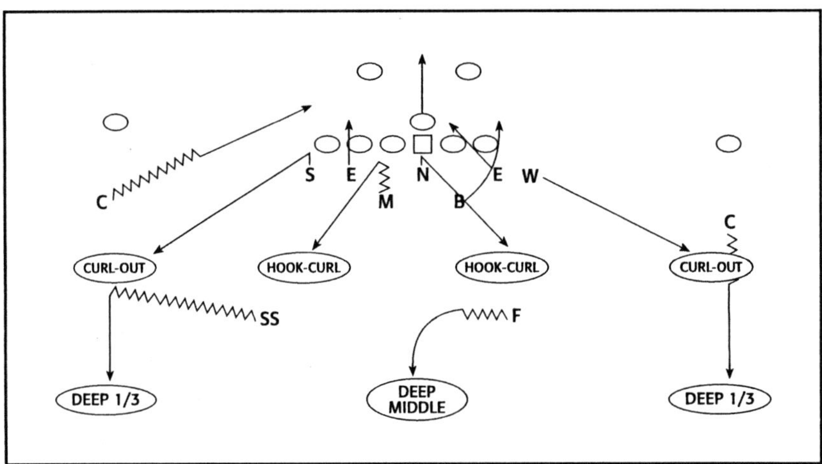

STUNT DESCRIPTION: This stunt features a strong-cornerback blitz and incorporates zone blitz principles into its scheme.

SECONDARY COVERAGE: This is a 4-under/3-deep zone. Stud, Mike, nose, and Whip drop off into the under coverage.

STRONG SAFETY: Lines up in a cover 2 disguise. As the cornerback moves inside, the strong safety moves to a position that enables him to cover the deep outside third at the snap.

STUD: Plays 9 technique versus run. Drops curl-out versus pass.

STRONG END: Plays 5 technique versus run. Contains the quarterback versus pass.

MIKE: Creeps toward the line as though he's going to blitz. Secures the B gap versus run and drops hook-curl versus pass.

NOSE: Plays 0 technique versus run. Drops weakside hook-curl versus pass.

BUCK: Blitzes through the outside shoulder of the offensive tackle, secures the C gap, and contains the quarterback.

WEAK END: Slants across the offensive tackle's face into the B gap.

WHIP: Plays 9 technique versus run. Drops curl-out versus pass.

FREE SAFETY: Lines up in a cover 2 disguise and drops to the deep middle third at the snap.

STRONG CORNER: Lines up in a cover 2 disguise. Moves to the inside during cadence and blitzes from the edge. He has a chance to make a big play!

WEAK CORNER: Lines up in a cover 2 disguise but moves to a position during cadence that enables him to cover the deep outside third.

STUNT #99

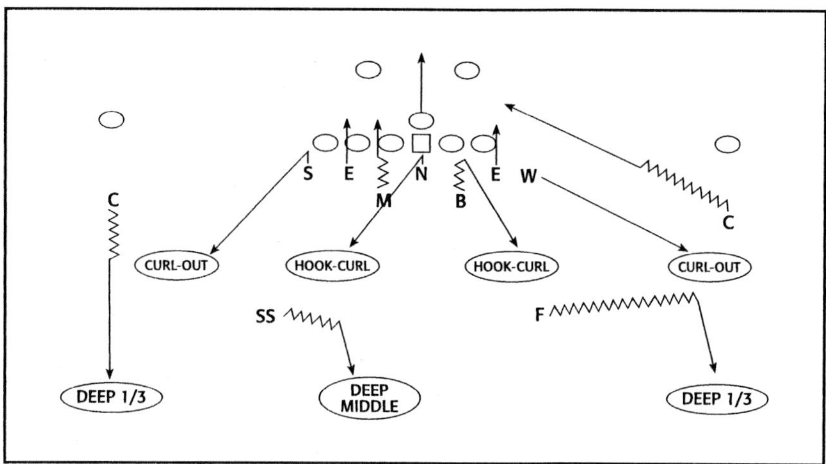

STUNT DESCRIPTION: This stunt features a weak-cornerback blitz and incorporates zone blitz principles into its scheme.

SECONDARY COVERAGE: This is a 4-under/3-deep zone. Stud, nose, Buck, and Whip drop off into the under coverage.

STRONG SAFETY: Lines up in a cover 2 disguise and drops to the deep middle third at the snap.

STUD: Plays 9 technique versus run. Drops curl-out versus pass.

STRONG END: Plays 5 technique versus run. Contains the quarterback versus pass.

MIKE: Blitzes through the outside shoulder of the offensive guard and secures the B gap.

NOSE: Plays 0 technique versus run. Drops strongside hook-curl versus pass.

BUCK: Creeps toward the line as though he's going to blitz. Secures the B gap versus run and drops hook-curl versus pass.

WEAK END: Plays 5 technique versus run. Contains the quarterback versus pass.

WHIP: Plays 9 technique versus run. Drops curl-out versus pass.

FREE SAFETY: Lines up in a cover 2 disguise. As the cornerback begins moving inside, the free safety must move outside and be in a position to cover the deep outside third at the snap.

STRONG CORNER: Lines up in a cover 2 disguise but moves to a position during cadence that enables him to cover the deep outside third.

WEAK CORNER: Lines up in a cover 2 disguise. Moves to the inside during cadence and blitzes from the edge. He has a chance to make a big play!

STUNT #100

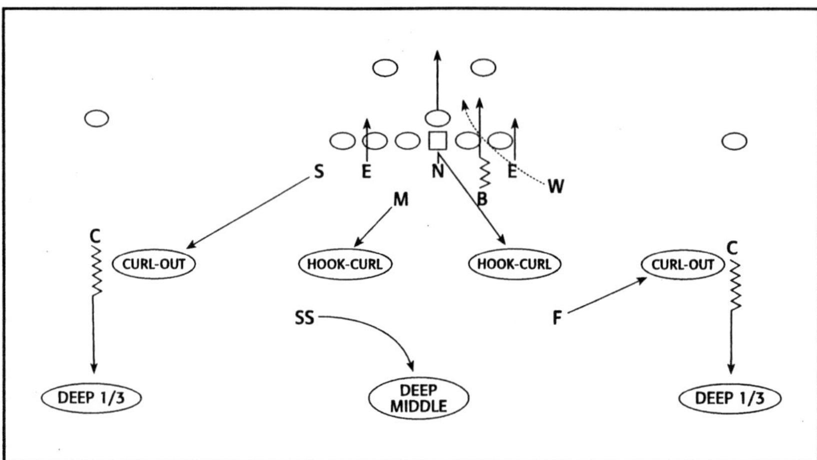

STUNT DESCRIPTION: This stunt features a delayed twin stunt and incorporates zone blitz principles into its scheme.

SECONDARY COVERAGE: This is a 4-under/3-deep zone. Stud, Mike, nose, and the free safety drop off into the under coverage.

STRONG SAFETY: Lines up in a cover 2 disguise and drops to the deep middle third at the snap.

STUD: Plays 9 technique versus run. Drops curl-out versus pass.

STRONG END: Plays 5 technique versus run. Contains the quarterback versus pass.

MIKE: Plays base technique versus run. Drops hook-curl versus pass.

NOSE: Plays 0 technique versus run. Drops weakside hook-curl versus pass.

BUCK: Creeps toward the line during cadence and blitzes through the outside shoulder of the offensive guard.

WEAK END: Plays 5 technique versus run. Contains the quarterback versus pass.

WHIP: Cheats back slightly. Plays 9 technique versus run. Delay blitzes (twin stunt) through the B gap versus pass.

FREE SAFETY: Lines up in a cover 2 disguise. Drops curl-out versus pass.

STRONG CORNER: Lines up in a cover 2 disguise, but moves to a position during cadence that enables him to cover the deep outside third.

WEAK CORNER: Lines up in a cover 2 disguise, but moves to a position during cadence that enables him to cover the deep outside third.

STUNT #101

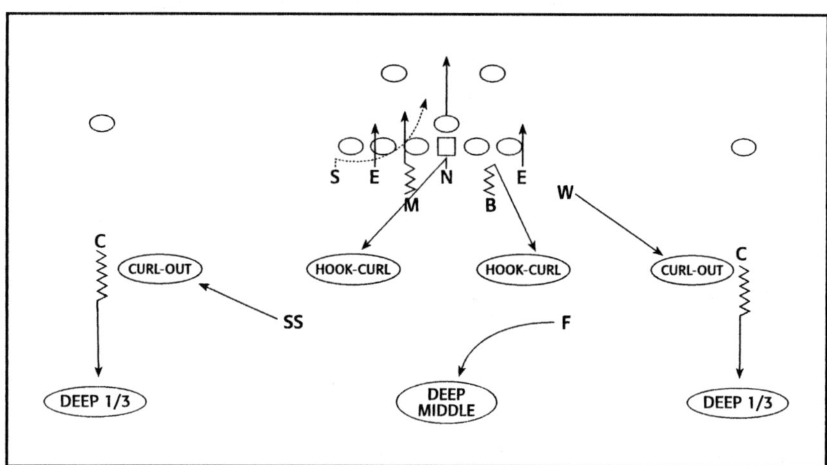

STUNT DESCRIPTION: This stunt features a delayed twin stunt and incorporates zone blitz principles into its scheme.

SECONDARY COVERAGE: This is a 4-under/3-deep zone. The nose, Buck, Whip, and strong safety drop off into the under coverage.

STRONG SAFETY: Lines up in a cover 2 disguise and drops curl-out versus pass.

STUD: Plays 9 technique versus run. Loops through the B gap (twin stunt) versus pass.

STRONG END: Plays 5 technique versus run. Contains the quarterback versus pass.

MIKE: Creeps toward the line during cadence and blitzes through the outside shoulder of the offensive guard.

NOSE: Plays 0 technique versus run. Drops strongside hook-curl versus pass.

BUCK: Creeps toward the line during cadence as though he intends to blitz. Secures the B gap versus run and drops hook-curl versus pass.

WEAK END: Plays 5 technique versus run. Contains the quarterback versus pass.

WHIP: Plays 9 technique versus run. Drops curl-out versus pass.

FREE SAFETY: Lines up in a cover 2 disguise. Drops to the deep middle third.

STRONG CORNER: Lines up in a cover 2 disguise, but moves to a position during cadence that enables him to cover the deep outside third.

WEAK CORNER: Lines up in a cover 2 disguise, but moves to a position during cadence that enables him to cover the deep outside third.

ABOUT THE AUTHOR

Leo Hand is the defensive coordinator at El Paso (TX) High School, a position he assumed in 2001. Prior to that, he held the same job at Irvin High School in El Paso, Texas. With over 33 years of experience as a teacher and coach, Hand has served in a variety of coaching positions in his career. At each stop, he has achieved a notable level of success.

A graduate of Emporia State University in Emporia, Kansas, Hand began his football coaching career in 1968 as the junior varsity coach at McQuaid Jesuit High School in Rochester, New York. After two seasons, he then accepted the job as the offensive line coach at Aquinas Institute (1970-'71). Next, he served as the head coach at Saint John Fisher College–a position he held for two years. He has also served on the gridiron staffs at APW (Parrish, NY) High School (head coach); Saint Anthony (Long Beach, CA) High School (head coach), Daniel Murphy (Los Angeles, CA) High School (head coach), Servite (Anaheim, CA) High School (head coach); Serra (Gardena, CA) High School (head coach); Long Beach (CA) City College (offensive line and linebackers); and Los Angeles (CA) Harbor College (offensive coordinator).

During the six-year period he spent coaching interscholastic teams in California, Hand's squads won 81 percent of their games in the highly competitive area of Southern California. At Serra High School, his teams compiled a 24-1 record, won a CIF championship, and were declared California State champions. On numerous occasions, he has helped rebuild several floundering gridiron teams into highly successful programs. For his efforts, he has been honored on numerous occasions with Coach-of-the-Year recognition.

A former Golden Gloves boxing champion, Hand is a prolific author, having written several football instructional books and numerous articles that have been published. He and his wife, Mary, have nine children and seven grandchildren.